THE
INFINITY
PRINCIPLE

ANSWERING THE
MYSTERY OF ONENESS

JANN DEWIT

BALBOA.PRESS
A DIVISION OF HAY HOUSE

Balboa Press books may be ordered through booksellers or by contacting:

Balboa Press
A Division of Hay House
1663 Liberty Drive
Bloomington, IN 47403
www.balboapress.com
844-682-1282

Because of the dynamic nature of the Internet, any web addresses or
links contained in this book may have changed since publication and
may no longer be valid. The views expressed in this work are solely those
of the author and do not necessarily reflect the views of the publisher,
and the publisher hereby disclaims any responsibility for them.

The author of this book does not dispense medical advice or prescribe
the use of any technique as a form of treatment for physical, emotional,
or medical problems without the advice of a physician, either directly
or indirectly. The intent of the author is only to offer information
of a general nature to help you in your quest for emotional and
spiritual well-being. In the event you use any of the information in
this book for yourself, which is your constitutional right, the author
and the publisher assume no responsibility for your actions.

Any people depicted in stock imagery provided by Getty Images are
models, and such images are being used for illustrative purposes only.
Certain stock imagery © Getty Images.

Print information available on the last page.

ISBN: 979-8-7652-5502-5 (sc)
ISBN: 979-8-7652-5503-2 (e)

Library of Congress Control Number: 2024917742

Balboa Press rev. date: 10/01/2024

This book is dedicated to my loving family, to my beloved friends, and to everyone on the path of discovery. May it stir some lust to further contemplate our purpose in this world.

Contents

Visionary mountain, above and afar. Like answers to questions, on life, love, and the longing to survive.

—Joan Armatrading,
'Visionary Mountain' [1]

Let go thy hold, Sannyasin bold. Say, 'Om, Tat Sat, Om!'

—Swami Vivekananda,
'The Song of the Sannyasin' [2]

Do I disturb, said he, as he knocked and came in. Not only do you disturb, said she, you shake my very existence. Welcome!

—Eeva Kilpi.
'Let me know if I disturb' [3]

Prologue

In 1975, I was a young lad of sixteen and had just started to roam the streets of my hometown, exploring the city and its people. One morning I met a man on the curb; he was definitely my elder, but our conversation was friendly and open-minded, and he listened to my thoughts with mindful respect. I don't recall exactly what was said, but I must have exposed ideas about life, the world, and how it was all put together. In other words, the kind of thoughts that constantly flowed through my mind as I watched the world revolve around me.

'Aah', my newfound friend said at one point, 'the eternal questions'.

I was immediately struck by his words and replied, 'Eternal questions—are there eternal questions?'

The man smiled and said, 'Well, yes, they are called eternal questions, they are questions that really have no answer'.

I had not heard that particular phrase before and I was amazed. Here I was, having a great conversation with an intelligent, streetwise person, someone who was much my senior and who seemed to understand the world's behaviours down to its intimate tendencies.

And suddenly, a new and unbound territory emerged out of the blue. *Wow*, thought I, *eternal questions—how can it be?* Just the sound of it made my head spin. The world was not known, not in its entirety; there were riddles unsolved. And it was not just me who did not understand; nobody knew the answers. It explained the ongoing confusion in the world; but of course if nobody knew, it was a sudden peek into the great unknown, but at the same time it made sense.

I had always sensed a lack of logic in the information given about the world. Somehow it did not add up. Why were people so unhappy and troubled if they knew what was going on? We acted out as if we knew, but at the same time we were subjected to a universal ignorance. We, the people of the world, with all our great leaders and all our grand history, were like kids in a dark room looking for the light switch. Just to think—*nobody* knew! Awe had my young mind in its grip—awe, sided by a feeling of wanting to know, of needing to know. I felt that there must be an answer. It could not be un-understandable. It would not be right; it would not be fair! And what was more, if there were eternal questions, logically there must be eternal answers!

I thanked the man and strode my path with a new quest at hand.

Introduction

Hello, dear friends journeying space and time. I hereby bid you welcome to a thought-experiment that takes us to the deepest depths any existential investigation can hope for. You may ask, what is an existential investigation? Well, it is an inquiry about the true nature of reality. The infinity principle definitely matches such standards as it reveals the one single truth that underpins all other truths. We are talking about nothing less than one undeniable truth that explains our deepest mysteries. And the best of all, it is done in a clear and understandable manner.

We have come a long way as the human species, sharing the ancestral lineage of mankind. (Not man as in men, but man as in human.) For as long as we can trace the evolution of our species, we have turned to our intellectual ability in order to make sense of our world. The term *intellectual* is not meant in any complicated way here. On the contrary, it simply points out that we naturally use our minds to logically describe our world and put our experiences into context in an intelligible way. Our intellects, our means of reasoning is the asset that place us in the special position we hold amongst organic life on this planet. This asset may have its faults, but nevertheless, one thing is undeniable: we cannot stop ourselves from wanting to understand our world.

As a young man, I was intrigued by a popular saying of the day. It read 'peace, love, and understanding'. Personally, I found the *understanding* part to be its most appealing element. I intuitively sensed that the notion of understanding held the key to answering our existential riddles and thereby enable us to heal our wounded world. The attraction of *peace* is obvious. Everyone wants peace. Even though we spend trillions of dollars on the war industry, we do it to maintain peace. Doubtlessly, selfishness, greed, and fear steer some of our decisions, which makes it seem as some parties deliberately want to go to war. But in the long run, everyone wants to live in peace. That is a given.

Love is equally obvious. Everyone wants love. If we had but one choice, and that choice stood between to love or to hate, everyone would choose love. That is a given too.

Understanding is a much subtler notion, since every attempt to logically understand the truth seems to end up in paradoxes. Yet, understanding is the key component in our ongoing attempts to achieve peace and love.

The enterprise of trying to understand the great truths about reality in a logical way has gone on for as long as we know. Let us remember Saint Anselm of Canterbury (1033–1109), who said, '*Credo ut intelligam,*' meaning, 'I believe in order to understand.' Saint Anselm was an educated scholar and a pious man.

Today, we tend to think that science and religion are opposites, but they are not. How could they be? They both try to understand the same reality, which also is the aim of this thought investigation.

Let me emphasize that the term *understanding* is crucial; let us reflect on what it means. Merriam-Webster dictionary describes it as 'The power to make experience intelligible by applying concepts and categories'. That is a concise and thorough description.

Yet we need to go deeper. Understanding reality is tricky. But even so, an intelligible understanding of reality is what the infinity principle has in store for us. The infinity principle tells us that we can understand the fundamental truths about this world. It goes on to tell us that the answer is close by, that we can reach it by our own merits, and that our deepest questions can be met without scientific knowledge or religious creed. The infinity principle sheds light on our most haunting paradoxes. It does not change reality at its core, which would be impossible since reality at such a level is unchangeable. But it helps us grasp the ground conditions that rule our journey through space and time. That is its promise as well as its inspiration.

Chapter 1

THE BEGINNING

*In which we start our journey towards
the deep end of reality.*

The infinity principle, as I have come to call it, first appeared before me as a sudden and unexpected insight, catching me dumbfounded in its profound simplicity. In the moment of revelation, it was wordless, yet all my questions fell into place. The idea as such arose out of an overlooked phenomenon, out of one single aspect about this world, whose value we, strangely enough, have failed to recognize up to this point. As an idea it is uncomplicated, yet it holds the capacity to dramatically enhance our understanding of our world.

What is existence, what is reality? That is what we ask here. How did it start, where will it end, what is its purpose, why does it seem paradoxical, and why is there evil and suffering in the world? These questions are answered by one simple insight. And not in a mysterious way but straightforwardly and absolutely in reason with our human minds. It does not provide any certain method or give any advice on how to solve personal issues on a detailed level. Neither does it explain specific mysteries such as where the vapour from vanishing black holes goes at the end of this universe. Such questions are interesting, but in the context of the infinity principle, they belong to the realm of details. And there are already thousands of books about details.

I am neither a mystic nor a scholar. I hold no degrees or fancy educations. I am a simple man, contributing to my family's livelihood working as a cook.

But neither mysticism nor scholarships are needed to comprehend what will be said here. On the contrary, everyone can understand the message given by the infinity principle. And yet it answers some of our deepest mysteries. The key lies within one small thing that has been overlooked and neglected for millennia. Well, if it is small, that might be discussed, and it cannot really be called a thing. It is a one-of-a-kind-phenomena, and it cannot be compared to anything else.

Yet without it there was nothing at all. We usually don't give it much attention, but that is about to change. According to the infinity principle, there is one single truth, one single piece of information out of which every other truth can be understood. It may sound too simple to be true, but the infinity principle is certain. We can call it a truth, or we can call it a notion. Either way, its contents are accessible to everyone.

We have all heard about it, but we have not properly appreciated its value. I am talking about nothing less than the notion of *infinity*. Now, infinity is usually treated as an insignificant player on the existential map, but such interpretation is a mistake. *Infinity* holds great overall significance, and as we explore its nature, it provides us with amazing insights, as well as explain our most sought-after riddles.

Let me start by asking you what the opposite of infinity might be. Let that sink in for a moment. You may or may not find an answer in your mind. Either way is fine; we just keep it as a teaser for now. We will go deep into this riddle and find out how it underpins reality. When I say, 'Go deep,' it is not meant in a mysterious way. Some things in this world are mysterious; we all agree on that. But here, our aim is first to understand what is real and natural about reality in a comprehensible way. If that sounds too boring for you, let me ensure you that we will run into mysteries eventually. But first and foremost, we are interested in uncovering the credible truths that funds our world.

We seldom talk about infinity, and that is for several reasons. It is hard to comprehend, it does not have any practical use, and it does not call out for our attention. Infinity is subtle, and we might say that it lacks a strong identity. Yet without it we would not exist. And that is a fact that ought to raise anyone's curiosity.

So what is so special about infinity, since it does not do anything, we do not notice it, and we cannot even point to it? All these statements are true, even if it does have other qualities that we get to in a short while. But let me draw this to our attention straight away. We may not be able to point to it, but neither can we deny its presence. We know that it is there, and we can be certain that it won't go away. There will never come a time when infinity disappears. And that, my friends, cannot be said about very many things in this world. Even if infinity seem subtle and identity-less, it is the most prominent component of reality that we will ever encounter. Not only that, it means that it carries infinite strength. It carries an infinite force that is present within us and without us, twenty-four/seven. That power, that force, is our main subject of interest here.

The initial insight came to me as a sudden epiphany that instantaneously illumined the fundamental essence of our world. In the moment it was absolutely self-evident, even if I afterwards understood that as seen from an everyday point of view it appears as both abstract and obscured. Anyhow, in the initial moment it was absolutely clear that infinity is real and readily present and that this truth is undeniable. And from this one single truth followed an understanding of the unescapable conditions that will be discussed here.

Let me present you a concise, boiled-down version of the vision as a whole. It goes like this:

- Infinity exists, thus absolute nothingness does not exist.
- Absolute nothingness do not exist, thus absolute equilibrium does not exist.
- Absolute equilibrium do not exist, thus one force is stronger.
- One force is stronger, thus that force is positive.

It may sound like baloney at a first hearing, but the initial insight was indisputable, and I will explain what it means. For starters, we are not talking about a Hollywood-science-fiction-kind-of-strong-hero-fixing-all-our-problems solution. We are merely talking about a logical understanding of the nature of reality. This insight could actually have been expressed even more concisely than in the example above. It could simply have read 'All is one—and one is good.' That would cover the whole thing, but that wouldn't be understandable. And it most certainly would not have made much of a book.

Still, the message is the same. Infinity must be one, and since it is one, it is positive, per definition. According to the infinity principle, this is a fact, and I hope to be able to make it understandable. It may be that you reject this idea at first, but bear with me; I assure you that it will be worth the effort.

Our mission then is to unveil the treasures hidden within the abstract notion that we call infinity. We have all heard the expression *All is One*, and even though we have a vague feel about what it means, we cannot fully grasp it. Now, this is to be expected. Understanding oneness by our ordinary, everyday thinking is quite impossible. Yet—which is what this book will demonstrate—it is still possible to get a pretty close understanding about it when presented with the right pieces of evidence.

The term oneness in itself implies something uncomplicated. I mean, honestly, what could be more uncomplicated than *one*? It is self-evident as such. But at the same time, which has been repeatedly demonstrated throughout the history of existential inquiry, discussing it, or trying to describe it, soon becomes a tricky business. And why is it so? Well, there are some obvious reasons.

When I started to look for ways to describe the message of the infinity principle, it became evident that in order to talk about oneness, it had to be split in two. It is the only way that we can even discuss it. Not because of our inability to comprehend abstract notions, but for a very rudimentary reason: All is one; that is a simple and straightforward statement. But to talk about it, there must be two. There must be the talker and the talked about, the watcher and that which is being watched

Already here we have a division. Already here we have 'two-ness'. And already here our minds start slipping into a deceptive territory.

So I decided to be proactive. In order to discuss, describe, and understand oneness, we will deliberately divide it into two. And we will pronounce it as this; reality is one, but it has two sides. Nothing more than that, very plain, very simple, very straightforward.

It can be likened to a coin with its two flipsides. The two sides are different from one another, but they constitute the same coin, the same one whole. Of course, in today's digitalized world, a coin may be an outdated simile, and maybe we should liken it to a cellphone. A cellphone also has two sides: one personal/changing side, and one impersonal/unchanging side. It is quite natural, and it is actually how we comprehend the world on an everyday basis. On one hand we experience the world of matter, as it is solidly presented before us. And at the same time we are aware that there is more to reality than meets the eye.

Anyhow, I will refer to these two sides as the *personal* side on one hand and the *impersonal* side on the other. The personal side we all know from our personal lives, which is how we look at the world from our own perspective. The impersonal side, on the other hand, we usually do not give much thought.

These expressions, the personal and the impersonal, I borrowed from the Vedic thought-tradition, and I will tell you how I came to make that choice. A while back I had the honour to talk to Swami Satyamayananda of the Vedanta Society of California[4], and among other things I asked him about the Vedic approach on God. He said that Vedanta traditionally describes God as having two sides, a personal and an impersonal side. This resonated with me, and the more I thought about it, I came to realize that everything in this world can be viewed from either a personal or an impersonal angle. I thus decided to use these terms to describe the infinity principle.

Now, this is what we will do here: we will set out on an existential conquest. We will emerge upon an existential inquiry where our aim is to intellectually connect the physical and the metaphysical sides of reality. This is surely not a new enterprise amongst human beings. Since the dawn of history, women and men alike have looked up to the stars, or into their hearts, asking for the purpose of this world. Yet, and you might say strangely enough, not very many understandable conclusions have been presented. One almost starts to wonder if we prefer to keep the mystery before answering it. I come to think about our children, who at a certain age ask *why* indefinitely. It always reaches a point where we as parents are forced to give up, telling our little darlings that we do not have the time to play this game right now. But one cannot help but wonder what would have happened if they were presented with a final and definite answer? Would it have stopped all progress? Would our curiosity about the world arrive at its end station? What do you say? Do we even want to find an answer? That is an interesting question, but I suggest that we leave it open for now; we will have an opinion in place before we reach the end of this story.

Chapter 2

SCIENCE

In which we are reminded to not look over
yonder for a truth that is present right here.

As we go about this thought-investigation, it will appear
that I disagree with the scientific method at times. This
is both true and untrue. The scientific method helps and
enhances our technical advancements and our knowledge
of the world to such extent that we all must stand in awe
before its wonders. Yet the infinity principle will show us
that when it comes to understanding reality at its deepest
level, we do not need the scientific method. Why? The
notion of infinity is self-explanatory. This means that we
need neither religious belief nor science. The unbuilt truth
that infinity reveals speaks for itself.

Today, science has almost become our new religion
and might be questioned in an almost similar way as
science itself has questioned religion in its own turn.
The world-famous scientist Stephen Hawking, and other
scholars from the scientific field, say that not only religion
is passed over by science, philosophy is too. Philosophy

is dead, Stephen Hawking says in the book *The Grand Design* (Hawking, Mlodinov, 2010)[5], claiming that science is the means that will give us all the answers.

And even if such a statement may be true to some extent, it will not be true when it comes to understanding infinity. The scientific method is to seek measurable, comparable, and verifiable proof. But infinity, or the notion of oneness, cannot be measured or compared. Hence, they cannot be verified by scientific standards. Thus, the scientific method is disqualified per definition in these matters.

Despite what anyone might say, infinity is undeniable. So let us be clear about this distinction between scientific thought and plain understanding right from the start. We must recognize what we are asking for. Stephen Hawking made astonishing calculations that indicate what are called *singularities* and are expected to be found within black holes, possibly the same kind of singularity that our universe might have emerged out of (and into which it might disappear one day).

Be how it may, Stephen Hawking sought the origin of the universe, which is a fantastic and honourable endeavour. But it is not the same as finding the origin of existence. Science may eventually be able to prove how the universe came to be by the help of particle colliders and advanced telescopes, but that does not give answers to an existential inquiry. There is a difference here. Whilst science tries to know reality scientifically, and religion stays with its beliefs, the infinity principle falls in the middle. Beyond scientific measurements and beyond religious belief, we can understand the core principles of reality using our own inherited wisdom and reasonable understanding. And that is what the infinity principle is here to help us with.

The three main authorities that historically have ventured to explain reality are *philosophy, religion, and science.* And they appear precisely in that order. Philosophy must have been first, since asking the why, how, and when questions are philosophical enterprises to begin with. The problem with philosophy is that even if it often finds the intriguing questions to ask, it seldom delivers satisfactory answers in any final sense. There is always a new why, how, when, or what waiting around the corner.

That is where religion steps in, telling stories with definite answers. The problem with religion, however, is that even though their stories contain great wisdom, they lack lasting logic and thus become a source of doubt. Religion has uncertainty built into the system, a certain factor of doubt. And this uncertainty, this doubt is covered up by rules and regulations, even condemnation.

Which is where science steps in. The scientific method illumines the discrepancies within religious explanation by proving the age of the universe, the mechanism of evolution, and so forth. Hence, religious supremacy has declined, and science has gotten on top of the game. And what is the problem with that? Well, as already said, science is great in doing what it is doing, in accordance with its own methods and principals. The scientific method of thorough examination and reasoning followed by verifying experimental conclusions works wonders. But when reality as an infinite whole is contemplated, then science breaks down. The scientific method relies on our five senses: sight, hearing, touch, smell, and taste. Beyond these measurements, science says, we cannot prove it; we cannot know it; it does not exist. Maybe I am a bit too harsh here. It is also true that science allows for wild ideas, and that some scientists burn with the desire to reach further still. But scientific thought is in itself dogmatic when it comes to metaphysical issues, and that becomes a problem when we aim to understand existence as a phenomenon.

From the infinity principle's point of view, the scientific method deals with understanding the details. And the details all take place within the personal field, in the realm of change. It is not that the details are uninteresting; on the contrary, they are very interesting, but they are also continuously changing. No matter how far we go, what fantastic new discoveries we make, how many universes we theoretically dream up, beyond every detail, beyond every personal conclusion a new door opens. That is how the personal realm works. That is the nature of the realm of details.

To understand reality fully, we must understand that which does not change. And that is what the infinity principle shows us. Let me put it this way: There is a difference between knowing and understanding. Certain things can be understood even if they cannot be known, and then I mean known in a scientific way. We all understand that infinity is infinite. But we don't know how we know. It cannot be measured; it cannot be compared to anything else, and it cannot be recognized by sight, hearing, smell, touch, or taste. Still, we know, we understand intuitively that it cannot be any other way.

The notion of infinity has an abstract, limitless logic. And the understanding of this holds the very key to the full understanding of reality.

So it appears that philosophy, religion, and science all make the same mistake. They mix the personal and impersonal sides of the coin. And that does not work when we want to intelligibly understand the fundamental truth about reality. To investigate the full nature of reality in an intelligible way, we must separate the two sides. The personal side talks about the details, and the impersonal side describes the underlying principles.

But whilst talking about science, let us challenge it further still. The most intriguing existential question is said to be, 'Why is there something rather than nothing? Why is there anything at all?'[6] The question is thoroughly investigated in the book *Why Does the World Exist?* (Holt 2013)[7], where philosopher Jim Holt gathers information from both historical and contemporary thinkers amongst all fields.

Another example is Robert Kuhn's 'Closer to Truth series'[8]. Robert too poses this question to scholars of all categories. Even Stephen Hawking calls it the ultimate question (Hawking, Mlodinow, 2011)[9]. And sure enough, the question, 'Why is there something rather than nothing?' inevitably pops up at some point when reality is thoroughly cross-examined. Strangely enough though, neither Hawking nor any other of the scientists and thinkers referred to in the above-mentioned publications seem to be able to deliver a straight answer. This is frustrating to every sincere truth seeker, but at the same time it is a bit cool since it leaves us with the pleasure to solve the mystery by ourselves.

And that is, in fact, what we will do here. This very question, 'Why is there anything rather than nothing?' will be readily, clearly and logically answered by the infinity principle.

But before we get to that, there is more to say about science—the hard problem of consciousness, for instance. The term is coined by scientist and philosopher David Chalmers[10], and it tells us that even if we scientifically can measure how neurons in our brains react to stimuli of the senses, it does not say how we experience our personal selves. Internally, we know that we are a self, that we are persons, and that we experience the world in a personal and unique way. We know what we mean by experiencing from our own point of view the colours, scents, associations, memories, feelings, and connections it gives rise to. But the personal experience, the personal self, cannot be shown on a screen. David Chalmers recognizes this, and he calls it the hard problem of consciousness. We know that the self is there, but we cannot scientifically describe it.

This issue is increasingly relevant in this day and age when we have started to construct artificial intelligence (AI) that can construct robots that themselves can build new robots. If this works out well, which we have reason to believe, these robots will become more successful in multiplying themselves than we ourselves could ever hope for. These robots can then conquer other planets in our solar system, and who knows what else. The question arises as to whether the progress of robots is a better choice out of an evolutionary perspective. I mean, if robots can achieve our wildest dreams more effectively than we can ourselves, what do we need ourselves for? Whatever we think of evolution, and whatever we think of technological possibilities, it raises the question of the self and the true meaning of progress. Does AI have a self? Is AI on a journey towards personal fulfilment? What is a personal self to begin with? These are questions that keep alluring us. Meanwhile, we can be sure of one thing: the realm of changingness will continue to change, but the infinite side of reality will not.

Theoretical physicist and Stanford professor Leonard Susskind[11] has said that as seen from where we stand on planet Earth, our universe expands faster than the speed of light. It means that the information beyond a certain point travels away from us faster than it can be sent back. The rays of light, and thereby the information sent from these distances will never reach us since they are moving away faster than their emitted light can travel back towards us. Which means that even if we could travel at the speed of light, we would not be able to catch up. Thus, it is *unknowable* to the scientific method.

Unknowable is a rather interesting term. It does not say that we don't know the answer just yet, it says that we will never know. It is downright impossible. At least in a scientifically measurable way. But we, the common people, we know that something is there, even beyond what we can scientifically know. We know it through sheer common sense. So the term unknowable tells us that we cannot know all the details of the changing personal realm. And science agrees on that. Still, we know that something is there because common sense tells us. And here the infinity principle will be our guide. The utility of the infinity principle is making us understand the nature of reality beyond the boundaries of scientific knowledge and religious faith.

Chapter 3

THE BIG WHY

Meet the hero of our story, the very
originator of our quest for truth.

At some point, every detective story, every relationship drama, every conflict between nations must try to establish what went wrong and who's to blame. Seeking the cause is essential in any investigation, and it is likewise true for an existential inquiry. Yet here it is a bit peculiar since we do not really need to know. I mean, why are we so eager to find out? Our lives do not depend on it. We cannot blame flight or fight response here. When we look around our world, we can clearly see that animals and plants don't ask why. They simply follow their instincts. But not us. Somewhere down the evolutionary path we developed the idea—the pledge, even—to question existence, more so now than ever as we spend billions and trillions trying to find out how life began, how the earth came to be, and how the universe sprang into action.

But as said, it is kind of peculiar when you think about it—why do we want to know? This is one of the great mysteries that was mentioned in the first chapter, and it is an intriguing question with great depth and great significance. Why do we want to know? Does it hint that existence has reasons beyond mere survival? Survival is our number-one driving force. We will talk more about that in a later chapter, and it will get pretty deep. But before we get that far, we shall first make an imaginary time travel back through our own footsteps.

Once upon a time, one of our ancestors posed the question *why* for the very first time. What caused this event we cannot know. It might have sprung out of frustration, or it might have sprung out of awe. We cannot know, but whatever caused it, it opened a new perspective upon this earth. We can call this unique and unprecedented occasion 'The Big Why', and we can recognize that we are still in the wake of its influence. This initial *why* opened a door to a whole new field of inquiry. No longer was it only about how and where we should eat and mate; suddenly we stood face to face with a deeper question.

The why question is unique to our species and a vital piece in the making of our humanity. Ever since this original why was uttered, we have been seekers in search of a secret mystery. We are on a mission to find the purpose of our journey through space and time. As the question has been unleashed, it cannot be taken back. We cannot stop ourselves from wondering at this point. If the first why hadn't been posed, we unknowingly kept obeying the physical rules of survival, just like the rest of organic life. But for some reason our journey took another route, and we passed the point of no return. Pandora's box was ripped open and could not be closed again. The genie got out of the bottle and would not get back in. The Gordian knot had to be unknit. Some people say that there is no answer and that we seek in vain, but then we ought to stop our search right now, because why seek something we do not expect to find? We might just as well admit it: we all want to answer the Big Why.

But what is it that we are asking? In *The Hitchhikers Guide to the Galaxy* (Adams 2012)[12], two young earthlings adrift on a spaceship get in contact with a supercomputer. The computer knows everything, and they are welcomed to ask anything. So they ask, 'What is the question of life, the universe, and everything?'

After some hard computing, the machine delivers its answer, which annoyingly enough simply reads, '42'.

The two earthlings are upset and loudly announce, 'We do not understand the answer!'

But the computer simply and matter-of-factly replies, 'That is because you do not understand the question.'

Douglas Adams, the author of this hilarious tale, may be accused of taking an easy way out here, but at the same time he puts his finger on something quite crucial. If we want to find the right answer, we must know what to ask for. So there we have another checkpoint on our agenda.

Chapter 4
THE WORD

*We recognize the connection between thoughts
and words and thereby expand our vision.*

Thought is prior to language; language couldn't possibly be prior to thought. Just as infants have thoughts before they know any words, in the same way we had thoughts before any language developed. It means that we can understand things, even abstract phenomena, before we have words to describe the understanding. Wordless thought is an interesting topic, not the least in the context of the infinity principle as this very idea first appeared as a wordless epiphany without having any outspoken explanation attached.

Yet, and amazingly enough, it contained impeccable truth. But even so, one cannot explain an idea intelligibly without dressing it in words, no matter how simple the idea might be. And then we find ourselves in a situation where we must ask ourselves which words to use. I have tried to find a consistent and understandable language. Whether I have succeeded can only be answered by you, the reader. I beg for your open-mindedness here, but at the same time I strongly emphasize that I reject slippery fuzziness and undetermined logic.

We will span a great mass of thought-history in the coming chapters, and at many times it will have to be rather briefly put, or this book could not have been written. Still, I have found it of interest to give room for a variety of ideas.

But the main topic will be a deep existential inquiry, with its head concern to find a logical understanding of reality as such. It will by necessity address abstract notions, and I realize that what seems logical to me may not seem similarly obvious to anyone else. So, to put us on a common track, I will address some thoughts around the vocabulary I have come to choose. Hopefully, it helps our shared understanding.

Reality

Our main word here is reality. Explaining reality in the capacity of being one all-inclusive whole is our main mission. The term reality can be used in many ways, but here it has its very precise definition. Here it is the chosen name for the *all-inclusive infinite whole*. It can easily be compared to the Sanskrit term *Brahman*[13], which also represents the infinite whole. But the term Brahman appears as strange for those who are unfamiliar with the Vedic tradition, and to be honest, it can be difficult even for those who are familiar with this specific line of thought, as it may seem to point towards an entity in a far-off distance. To be sure, the infinite whole is not an entity, and neither is it far-off. Rather, it is right here, and with everything included. Thus, I find reality to be a more direct term. Reality, as the term is used here, is claimed to include everything unlimitedly. When I started to look for what term to use, I at first fancied the term *existence*. But then I realized existence primarily refers to what we experience through our five senses; thereby, it does not cover what is beyond that. Furthermore, in its original Latin meaning, existence translates to 'that which stands out'. And reality, as the term is used here, does not stand out. It is rather that in which all the standing out happens. Another option was the term *creation*, but according to the infinity principle, reality has never been created, and thus the term creation was not suitable. This doesn't mean there is no creating going on within reality. On the contrary, there is lots of creating going on, but only on the personal side. Reality as such is not created. This is due to a very simple reason: reality is infinite, and as such, without beginning.

Illusion

To emphasize what I just said, we may note that many existential descriptions use the word illusion to describe certain aspects of reality. I actually heard one debater who more or less described existence as such: 'An apparent appearance apparently appears to appear', in other words, existence is an illusion. That is one way to see it; it must not be wrong. However, in this text, illusions are part of our one reality. Things may appear as illusionary, but that doesn't mean that they are unreal. In other words, things may seem unreal but still be part of reality. Later in this text we will come across a notion that cannot be—namely, nothingness. This concept, nothingness, will be referred to as *not real*, rather than unreal, a note that may seem of minor relevance but which will show to have significant importance.

Personal versus Impersonal

So reality is one whole, but that is not how we experience it. We experience reality as multilayered and complex. And right here we confront our very enigma! This is the mystery that we are trying to solve. How can we ever understand the concept of oneness when all we see is diversity? Well, there is an answer. We do it by describing reality as having two sides, the personal and the impersonal side.

Changing versus Unchanging

The two sides have separate attributes, and we can recognize that the personal side changes whilst the impersonal side does not. The personal side is in a state of constant flux and changes all the time. That is its very nature.

The impersonal side, on the other hand, never changes. In fact, reality as seen from the impersonal side cannot change. It is impossible since it already contains everything. So we face the puzzling conclusion that our one reality is both changing and unchanging simultaneously. This puzzle has teased humankind for ages, and luckily we are now on the track towards a clearer understanding, an understanding that springs from allowing ourselves to describe our one reality as having two sides, namely both changingness and unchangingness.

Truth

Another way to notice the difference between the two sides is the concept of truth. On the personal side, truth varies depending on perspective, but on the impersonal side, it does not vary at all. Personal truth is dependent, whilst impersonal truth is independent. Personal truth changes due to circumstances. Impersonal truth don't change at all. This do not mean that personal truths are untrue; they are true in their place and time. They will inevitably change, not because they are wrong in the first place, but because they are subject to time and thus bound to change. Personal truths are like opinions: we are all entitled to our opinions, but opinions vary depending on perspective. That is the difference. Impersonal truths are not subject to time and do not vary. Impersonal truths are true *all the way down*.

It is like the story about the lady who in front of her teacher exclaimed that the world is situated on the back of a giant turtle.

The teacher asks her, 'What is beneath the turtle?'

The lady replies, 'Ha. You think you are very clever, young man, but there are turtles *all the way down*.'

It is a fun story, but the query is real. What is fundamental truth? One could argue that a fundamental truth cannot be altered or changed. It cannot be subject to fear of being overruled, cancelled, or empowered by another truth. Such are the characteristics that would be needed to fully render being titled fundamental. Now, is there such a truth? Well, I say that there is. The ultimate infiniteness of reality fulfils all the qualifications.

Metaphysics

The term metaphysics fits perfectly with our reasoning here. The term stems from the work of Aristotle. Aristotle contributed largely to our description of the physical world, but he also turned his attention to what goes on beyond the physical realm. *Meta* means after, or beyond, in Greek, and thus metaphysics implies another step after understanding the physical world. It deals with issues that can be imagined but cannot be known through our five senses. Metaphysics opposes ordinary physics, and opposites are always interesting as they provoke our mindset to broaden its vision. The concept of metaphysics points out that reality is divided into two realms, one that we can see, hear, touch, smell, and taste, and one we cannot. This concept is in perfect alignment with the infinity principle as it naturally points out that reality has two sides: physical and metaphysical.

Logic and Inevitability

The infinity principle gets explained through logical reasoning. What do I mean by logical reasoning? Well, let us start investigating this subject through three types of logic that are mentioned in the Vedic tradition. First, we have *Tarka*, which means logical reasoning where one thought leads to another in an uninterrupted fashion. And then we have *Kutarka*, which means wrong logic, or logic that proves fault in the world, thereby justifying blame, and thereby leading astray from infinite truth. And lastly, *Vitarka* goes beyond ordinary logic and sees the world as it is, beyond the boundaries of the rational mind. The logic of the infinity principle is closest to the latter.

But the infinity principle also refers to an understandable reasoning leading up to an inevitable conclusion. Inevitability is an important factor. Infinity is inevitable and can therefore be called the logical core-principle of reality. Thus, we see that logical thinking can take us all the way to understanding the core of reality. And that is a fantastic thing.

But having said that, a logical approach can also appear as rather dry. Not that it is wrong, but it may seem 'too much in the head'. Sri-Sri Ravi Shankar, the founder of Art of Living, says in his Shiva Sutras Commentary (Sri-Sri Publication Trust 2010)[14] that reasoning and feelings are opposites. 'There is no logic in feelings, and there are no feelings in logic'. And he uses chanting mantras as an example. The logical mind thinks, *Why should I repeat the same mantra over and over again? Is it not enough to say it once?* But the practitioner who experiences devotion, bliss, and the joy of commitment does not agree. And it is said that a sincere emotional experience can be a direct way to self-realization. Yet I think that at the end of the day we are intellectual beings, and we need to find reason to be satisfied.

But then again, I may be wrong. My wife, for instance, does not agree with me here. To her it is more natural to trust her feelings. And I trust her, so what can I say?

Entity

This is tricky. As we try to grasp the personal vs the impersonal, we will inevitably reach a point where we must ask ourselves where the boundaries of a personal entity are drawn. We must ask ourselves two questions: What is a person? And what is an entity?

From a human perspective we have our picture of what a person is, and we usually agree that our bodies represent our personal selves. In that respect, we are entities. But if we take it further, what exactly is the boundary for our personal self? Where, how, and when does it start? Let us consider a cell. We are built by cells. First there is only one, and it splits into two, which splits into four, and so on. After only forty-eight splits, it amounts to some ten thousand trillion cells. It sounds unbelievable, but you can check it on your calculator. And that is just a very early stage of a human body.

Further still, each and every cell contains millions of particles that are used up and transformed by the minute in a totally unimaginable metamorphic process. The knowledge about cells, molecules, mitochondria, enzymes, and so forth we owe to the field of scientific research, and let us thank science for that.

But an existential inquiry must dig even deeper and ask about the boundary of a self. Is a cell a personal self on a personal journey? Spontaneously we would say no. Or what about germs? We have trillions of germs in our guts. Are they us? Are they personal entities, or are they just entities? A glass of water on the shelf is not us, but when we drink it, it becomes part of us. Where is the boundary of the self then?

What about a planet? Is a planet an entity? I think we all say yes to that. But is it a self? Not in any way that we can understand, but it is on a journey: it gets born, it has a lifespan, and it dies. And so does a galaxy. So is a galaxy an entity, or is it a cluster of entities? What about a universe? What about quarks? I do not mean to cause confusion, but it is tricky to nail down the self or to specify the boundary of an entity. So in an existential wordlist, the term entity, even if unsatisfactorily explained, has its rightful place.

Intuition

Intuition is interesting. It seems to be a mix of our evolutionary and social histories downloaded in our DNA and in our traditions. It also has a flavour of a God-given gift, a knowingness in the backs of our minds that allows us to know without knowing how we know. It may sound mysterious, but mysterious is not what is asked for here. It has nothing to do with foretelling the future or connecting with other dimensions. Such things may occur, but it is not part of the infinity principle. The infinity principle is not that interested in knowing who's on the phone before we pick it up, or things like that. Intuition is often looked upon as vague and untrustworthy, and that is not what we want here. We want to trust our minds' capability to understand the basic nature of reality. Intuition tells us self-evident things, such as being aware of reading this text for instance, which is self-evident to a degree that it doesn't need to be mentioned. Still I mention it, and that is to emphasize that reality is just as self-evident. We all have access to intuitive knowingness, whether we agree to such idea or not.

Take infinity again. We know that it is there, but how do we know? We know it intuitively. It may seem obvious, and sure enough, that is just what it is. Einstein famously said that imagination is greater than knowledge. I don't think he meant that fantasies are more accurate than knowingness, but I think that he pointed towards the fact that knowledge is by nature limited whilst imagination is not. He himself seems to have trusted a great deal in what he called intuition.

So what is intuition? Beyond our thinking capacity there is a wisdom and a logic. Valuable insights can be gained and even hard facts can be accessed through trusting reality at large whilst downplaying our own egoic ambitions.

Instinct

Instincts are our most compelling driving forces. Does it necessarily mean that they must be obeyed? Can there be evolutionary benefits beyond their limiting influences? Is it even possible that mankind's evolution spirals towards a future where some of our most basic instincts become obsolete? Instinct is a fascinating topic, and we will discuss it more before the end of this book.

Common Sense

We tend to treat common sense in a belittling manner. When something is referred to as common sense, it is supposed to be something that everyone should understand and hence it is not given the same status as scholarly knowledge. This is a mistake. The infinity principle holds common sense in high regard, and for the same reasons that it is usually belittled. The greatest mysteries of the world are obvious and self-evident when we allow ourselves to trust our inner knowingness. Scientific knowledge is highly efficient in so many ways but when it comes to answering the Big Why, common sense holds the upper hand, and thus we should honour and respect it.

Abstract and Paradoxical Ideas

The mere recognition of infinity's inscrutability gives answers to some of our greatest mysteries. It tells us that reality is one limitless whole. Now, that is indeed abstract, but at the same time it is indisputable. We need to realize that an existential inquiry cannot shy the abstract. It is abstract per definition.

So why do we have problems with the abstract? Well, abstract notions lack visual targets or final ending goals; thus, they cannot be fenced, and thus they put us in a state of uncertainty. Therefore, we shield ourselves by treating abstract notions as mere imagination. But they are not. The abstract may be difficult to measure, but it is still part of reality. Abstract notions point beyond our everyday vision, and that is where we must go to seek unchanging truth. As said, infinity is a great example of an abstract notion. We cannot measure it, but we know that it is there. According to the infinity principle, abstract notions are just as qualified components of reality as physical entities are, if not even more so.

Paradoxes are a bit similar to abstractions. They can be visualized, but their meaning can be difficult to point out. Paradoxes make us raise our brows and mildly shake our heads. We sense a hidden truth but fail to understand how it can be. Someone has said that God speaks to us in paradoxes. That is rather beautifully put. The term paradox is Greek, and it plays an important part in the early history of philosophy. For instance, the Greek philosopher Parmenides[15] proclaimed that all is one. Not surprisingly, his ideas were doubted. But he had a disciple, Zenon, who, to prove Parmenides right, constructed paradoxes for which he became famous. Much of the originals are lost in the stride of time but a few remain and can be found for anyone who is interested. One of these paradoxes says that every distance can be divided in two, and that it therefore is impossible to reach the end. We can only get to the next in-between state. He thereby shows that neither the moment nor the movement really take us anywhere. We are seemingly moving, but on a larger scale we never get anywhere. We never reach the wall; we are still within the one whole. It seems to say that since all is one, no one ever gets anywhere, which is logical as seen from an infinite viewpoint. Thus, Zenon presents us with a physical image that connects the personal and impersonal realms. (There are mathematical ideas that say the same thing, such as *The Cantor Set* by George Cantor, or the work of Benoir Mandelbrot who introduced the notion of *Fractals*.) Interestingly, the Zenon paradoxes are still being discussed by mathematicians, scientists, and thinkers, but without any consensus reached as yet.

Paradoxes are powerful because they point beyond our everyday awareness. And they may come across as rather hilarious. Let me give you a few examples.

The world is not perfect, because if it had been perfect, it had not been perfect. Can that be explained? Well, yes. The perfect must be compared to the imperfect in order to be known. If everything was perfect, the perfect had been neutral, and it had not been noticed. Thus must a perfect world be imperfect to be known as perfect.

Or even wilder: The obvious is obviously not obvious. It sounds ludicrous, but consider infinity. Is infinity obvious? We must agree that it is. Can we fully understand it? It seems that we cannot. Thus, it is obvious, and at the same time not obvious.

A third example would be our longing for freedom: To obtain freedom, there must be something to be free from, and when there is something to be free from, there is no freedom.

I do not say this to cause confusion. I say it to take us nearer to the truth. Paradoxes are tricky, but they point towards something essential. Everything in the world carries a tint of paradoxicality. Everything except infinity. Infinity as such is unparadoxical, which makes it the most trustworthy phenomena of all. It has no malicious tricks up its sleeve. (Even if that, paradoxically enough, is why we have such hard time understanding it in the first place.)

Meditation and Contemplation

Deep meditation is to not think. The mind is freed from prejudice and expectation, and ideas and answers appear in a spontaneous and relaxed manner. Meditation is a precious tool accessible to us all. It is often considered being mystical, but it must not be. According to what already has been said here, the infinity principle does not look for the mystical but focuses on connecting the two sides of reality into one understandable whole.

Meditation, or the act of quieting the thinking mind, allows access to Vitarka, which is the Sanskrit word for the natural logic that is to be found beyond our personal desires. It complies with what was said in the ingress to this chapter, thought without words, thinking without labels. In between our manifest thoughts we access the impersonal side. To put them into effect on the personal side, though, we must dress them in words. Such are the rules, it seems. But it is good to recognize the difference between these two ways of *thinking* as it broadens our perspective.

What more can be said about meditation? Well, if you ever heard about speed meditation, let me tell you that there is no such thing. It does not work that way. This does not mean that a meditative state cannot be entered quite instantly, or that meditation must go on for a long time. But it cannot be forced. This is a fact that may serve to remind us about a rather neglected side of existence. Silence is golden. In order to move beyond the Big Why, we need to stop our thinking minds and pause in the gap between thoughts.

Sufi poet Rumi[16] said, 'The language of God is silence; words are only poor translations.' Meditation where conceptual thoughts are muted helps us sense that voice of silence. It is not magical or mystical, it is plain and simple.

What about the term contemplation then? It is quite similar to meditation, but at the same time it is quite different. It takes place at the edges of the gap, one might say. It is more to be likened to pointed awareness.

Like meditation, it relies on a relaxed mind, but in contemplation, thoughts of concern are allowed to churn and filter. That is at least how I recognize the difference between these two methods.

The Vedic Tradition

I repeatedly refer to the Vedic thought-tradition, and let me tell you why. After first becoming aware of the infinite solution, I looked around for other aspects of this idea, and the Vedic tradition inhabits the mastery of this kind of existential investigation. For those who do not know, the Vedic thought-tradition is a wisdom-tradition stemming out of one of our oldest known societies, namely the Indus Valley civilization, which dates back at least five thousand years. These ideas have never died out and are still the foundation of the wisdom-tradition of India. Its roots are originally ascribed to wise sages called *rishis* and have to a large extent been passed on orally. The tradition as such does not have an outpointed leader, or a direct centre, which is probably a reason why it is so seldom commented on amongst western scholars. (Compare it to Buddhism for instance, which is much more acknowledged. Buddhism stem out of the same thought-tradition but has the Buddha as a central figure) This is a bit unfortunate because this vast tradition contains knowledge of the highest value. I believe an existential inquiry must include the Vedic tradition. At least it's wisdom-tradition, if maybe not so much the religious side of it.

Wisdom

An existential inquiry is per definition an epistemological enterprise. In other words, we ask ourselves how we know what we know. The notion of wisdom is a source of knowledge that deserves more respect than it gets. Wisdom links us to an inherited knowledge. We often cannot trace it, but still, we trust it. It has been called knowledge without emotional attachment, which is rather well put. It would imply that wise understanding is unattached by personal longing and desires and therefore more right to the point. Without trying to define wisdom in absolute terms, let us not forget its value in the evolution of mankind, and let us also recognize its significance as we keep looking for an overall purpose to life. The Native Americans for instance had a living relation to wisdom. It did not help them much in the competition with the Europeans, but their wisdom possessed valuable insights that we all can benefit from.

Disclaimer

Finally, a wordlist about oneness must by necessity include a disclaimer. And this is for a very specific reason. When we aim to articulate deeper truth using humanmade vocabulary, we must realize that no humanmade term can be absolutely accurate. For example, when we give oneness a name, we place it outside ourselves. We point towards it: it is over there. And when it is placed over there, and we are pointing towards it, it is no longer one, it is two, the seer and the seen. Thus, we cannot reach a full understanding merely by using terminology.

To fully understand oneness, we must accept that the two are one. And to do that, we must dissolve our personal selves into it. And when that is done, the urge to understand dissolves too, because when all secrets are known, the question disappears. As an old Vedic saying has it: 'Those who are not enlightened yet, they have the question but not the answer, whilst those already enlightened have the answer but not the question.'

It means that the closest we can get to understanding oneness from the personal point of view is *to understand what it is that we cannot understand.* Which is not that bad. But that is as close as we can get. At least without giving up our personality. And this is of course the reason why an existential inquiry is such a tricky business in the first place. Because we don't want to give up our personality quite yet, do we? At least not before we finished this book.

Chapter 5

INFINITY

In which we dive into the starry sky, pondering its end.

The infinity principle explains our deepest mysteries through one simple fact, namely that infinity is infinite. But what do we mean by infinite? Can we even define such a concept? Well, we can try.

Let me start by sharing my own first encounter with this magnificent and tantalizing phenomenon. It happened on a crispy wintry evening promenade with my mom. I was around eight or nine years of age. The starry sky was immense above our heads, and we were lost in amazement underneath its depth. I asked my mother where it ended, a natural question, so it seemed. But to my confusion, she said that it had no end. I am sure that she wanted to give a more precise answer, but she could not; she simply did not have one. And I cannot really blame her, can I?

Almost sixty years has passed, and I am still trying to find someone who can give a straight answer. But at the time I was baffled, so I took the question to my sister, who was always older and wiser than me (she still is, by the way). She confirmed that it was endless, adding the rhetorical question, how could it end? Would there be a wall? If so, what would be behind the wall? She must have seen the haunted disbelief in my eyes and wrapped it all up by saying that the human mind is unable to grasp infinity since everything we know of operates within limits.

I had no other authority to turn to at the time, and I had to take it as a truth. But I was not satisfied, and I kept it as an unsolved riddle in the back of my mind.

This anecdote is probably quite commonplace. I reckon we all have a first encounter with infinity stored somewhere in the backs of our minds. And I would say that my sister's explanation is quite commonplace too. We treat infinity as un-understandable; we file it as meaningless, and we leave it at that, not knowing what to do with it. But infinity is not meaningless. On the contrary, it is the stern opposite to meaninglessness. Without infinity, nothing else had been. Infinity is the most fundamental phenomenon of all, and thus it is the very essence of meaning.

Infinity equals logic absolute. Infinity cannot be altered, and not just because we don't have the means to alter it but because it cannot be altered per definition. Infinity is a fact, self-evident beyond all doubt, and as such it is common knowledge to us all. It is not a hidden secret. It is a logical truth in the deepest sense of the word because it cannot change. And why can't it change? Because it covers all and everything. Nothing can interfere with it. Nothing can be added, and nothing can be taken away. Furthermore, it covers everything limitlessly, and thus there is no other place it can go. Note that there cannot be two infinites. They simply would not fit alongside one another. Infinity is one and one only.

And so it cannot change, nor does it need to because it does not lack anything. It is absolutely self-sufficient, real beyond time and space, real even beyond eternity. Eternity, in its turn, is dependent on infinity and could not have been without it. So, in that sense, infinity is the ultimate platform, the chief principle of reality. Its only alternative would be nothingness, and nothingness, as will be clearly demonstrated in chapter eight, is impossible.

Ulf Danielsson, Swedish professor in physics, says in his book '*The Darkness at the End of Time*'(Danielsson, 2020)[17] that the term infinity is nothing but another word for saying that something is *really, really big*. He goes on to say that it is easy to get lost in philosophical ideas about what infinity is but that when we do, we miss the world of physics, which then is the same as missing the important stuff.

This viewpoint seems to be a common interpretation of infinity amongst hardcore physicists. According to the infinity principle, however, that is a rather discriminating thought, not to say, totally wrong. Infinity is not *really, really big*. The notion of infinity is not even that sort of measurement; in other words, it is not a distance. It cannot be compared to anything else and cannot be called big or small. It is not far away, and it is not close by. It is everywhere, and it is better likened to a fundamental state of beingness than a format amongst other phenomena. It is the most certain aspect of reality. In fact, it is its only necessary component. Everything else can be taken away, but not infinity. Mind and matter can go; neither are necessary, and infinity would be just as real even without them.

Physically, we live in a three-dimensional world where a line or a dot exemplifies the first dimension, a square exemplifies the second, and a cube exemplifies the third. It could be agreed to call infinity a dimension in its own right. It would be a dimension that stretches in every direction seamlessly, even going inwards, which of course is a bit difficult to comprehend. Difficult but not undoable.

Science finds infinity rather useless as it seems, but that doesn't mean that it is useless per se. In fact, it is rather the opposite to uselessness, since without it nothing else would be, not even the universe. The universe is a topic that science dearly examines, and one classic question is whether the universe is infinite. At the same time, the Big Bang Theory is still valid in such discussions. The infinity principle's comment would be that the universe cannot be infinite in one end and have a starting point in the other. It may have started at one point, and it may keep on endlessly in the other end—this we do not know, but that is not a description of infinity. If the universe has a starting point, then it is not infinite, period. Infinity is infinite in every direction. Yes, it is hard to grasp, but what would be the alternative, that it stops somewhere? As said, it is even infinite inwards, which is our most challenging thought, but I suggest that you try to imagine a place where it stops. You will find that you cannot even imagine it.

Scientific thought dismisses arguments about infinity and calls them philosophical. I call them real—as real as anything can be. Infinity might not be a thing that can be captured in a telescope, but it is unchangingly present within and without every aspect of reality. We cannot get our heads around it, as the saying so neatly has it, but neither can we deny it. Infinity is a fact, and it holds the key to an understanding of reality at core level.

Philosophy is a Greek term. It translates to *love of wisdom*. Some five hundred years before Christ, Greek philosophers abandoned old godly explanations, aiming to intelligibly explain reality through nature-oriented observations. Just like scientists today, they wanted to describe the fundamental building blocks out of which the world arises. Thales of Miletus, who has been called the first philosopher, suggested that everything comes out of water. Anaximenes, who was a bit later, slightly changed it, suggesting that everything comes out of air. Both these guys were brilliant thinkers and had lots of other ideas on their agendas, but it is clear that they tried to figure out how the world was made and from where it came.

There was another interesting guy, Anaximander, from the same area. He had ideas that correlate directly to the message of the infinity principle. He talked about an undefined core-substance, a state of beingness, which he called *apeiron*. Apeiron translates to infinite, limitless, boundless. According to Anaximander, apeiron was an unspecified state of beingness out of which everything emerged and also returned to.

And then there was Parmenides[18]. He said that everything is one, that oneness is real, and that it is the fundamental quintessence of reality. He said, 'That which is, must be, and that which is not, cannot be.' Which is more or less the exact words of the infinity principle.

And there were other philosophers from that time and age. There was Heraclitus, who talked about a fundamental truth, which he named logos. This is definitely interesting. The word *logos* is used in many ways, but its root form simply means *word*, or *meaning*. Heraclitus said, 'When not listening to me, but to logos, it is wise to agree that all is one.' He points to a truth that he calls logos; in other words, a truth that has no name, but which is there for all to see. A truth that reveals that all is one. Again, it is very close to the message given by the infinity principle.

These guys operated about twenty-five hundred years ago. But what about our contemporaries? What about our present time? Twenty-first-century philosopher Jim Holt, in his book *Why Does the World Exist?* (Holt 2013)[19], consults a vast number of thinkers. Among other ideas, he highlights three staples of modern western thought tradition.

Firstly, one idea was exemplified by seventeenth-century philosopher Gottfried Leibniz and his 'principle of sufficient reason', which roughly says that everything depends on something, which is similar to the law of cause and effect. The idea of cause and effect may seem obvious at first glance, but when scrutinized closely it shows to have great implications.

And as the second staple, Jim Holt points out 'the theory of everything', which is a scientific idea about a unified theory of the cosmos that hopes to combine classical physics and quantum physics.

And thirdly, Jim talks about simplicity, which is a

scientific ideal saying that the simplest definition is most likely to be true, which is similar to when mathematicians talk of beautiful equations, the simpler, the better (for example, $E=mc^2$).[20]

So now we all wonder what the infinity principle has to say about all this. Well, let us start with the latest input, namely the notion of simplicity. Throughout his book, Jim Holt stubbornly asks, 'Why is there something rather than nothing?' and gets more and more frustrated as nothingness keeps refusing to crystalize. Why is he frustrated? Well, nothingness must be the simplest form of all, and yet it cannot be scientifically tracked down. To Jim Holt this seems to come as a big surprise. Obviously, he had not heard about the infinity principle at the time.

Secondly, we confront the principle of sufficient reason, the matter of cause and effect. And again we ask, 'Why is there something rather than nothing?' And we recognize that when we do so, we simultaneously admit that there is something. And the principle of sufficient reason is lost. If everything is caused by a former event, what then caused the original something, what caused infinity? Well, here we have the Big Why in yet another outfit. And Jim Holt gets more and more frustrated as he keeps trying to answer, 'Why is there something rather than nothing?'

Lastly, we confront *the theory of everything*, which is all about a unified theory to explain the lot. At this point, Jim's philosophical side and scientific thought shares a common problem. No matter how well classical and quantum physics ever will be connected, it will still not answer the Big Why. Even if it was possible to find the very last detail of physics, we would still have to ask why that one piece was the last. There is no way to get around that dilemma. Luckily for us, the infinity principle does not have this problem.

So, what is the answer then? Why are we unable to track down the starting point? Why can't we find the first rung of the ladder? How does the infinity principle solve this enigma? The answer is as simple as can be. Whenever we ask *why*, we ask for a cause, a starting point, a beginning. And as infinity has neither, the problem dissolves into a non-issue. This may seem to be an even too simple answer, yet it is undeniable. Infinity has always been and therefore has not emerged out of something else. There never was someone who said, 'OK, it is time to create infinity.' To be sure, infinity has always been, and nothingness has never been. When we equal reality with infinity, we see that the why question is a non-issue.

I am sorry if it ruins anyone's sense of mystery, but the infinity principle is relentless at this point. Infinity is infinite; thus, reality has always been, and thus there is no why question to answer in that regard. This is the strictly logical answer to *why is there something rather than nothing*. For all of you who find this realization disturbing, it can be remembered that this is only true as seen from the impersonal side where we look at the big picture. On the personal level, in the world of details, there will always be a multitude of *whys* to answer, so the thrill won't go away.

Allow me to close this chapter by sharing a story about Albert Einstein. Someone told me that he tried to fit infinity into an early version of the relativity principle, but he found himself forced to leave it for other options. I am not sure if it is a true story, but it make sense anyhow. Einstein's mission was to explain the linking forces in the universe, and infinity does not link to anything. It is more like an independent backdrop. And what is more when we talk about Einstein; we all know that he used the speed of light as a constant in his calculations. Now, infinity is a constant if anything, and it is real to both the relativity principle and to the quantum field theory. I am not a scientist, but ... the theory of everything, anyone?

Chapter 6
THE WHOLE

Picturing reality as one whole.

We have talked about the phenomena called infinity and how modern science fails to recognize its true nature. We have also heard about antique Greek philosophical ideas about oneness.

Now we will consult another major player on the field of existential investigation who was on the ball long before the Greeks stepped into the arena. I am talking about the Samkhya tradition[21], the early Vedic wisdom tradition. I will share with you an example that I came across in a small bookstore in Mysore, India. It is a verse taken from a contemporary exposition of the ancient tale 'Ramayana', here edited and translated by C. Rajagopalachari[22]. It goes like this:

'What is whole; this is whole; what has come out of the whole is also whole. When the whole is taken out of the whole, the whole still remains whole.' (In Sanskrit, *'Om poornamadah poornamidam poornat poornamudachyate poornasya poornamaadaaya poornamevaavasishyate.'*)

This is surely a neat example of abstract thinking. But can we understand it? Well, as always, we can try.

Let us begin by defining what is meant by the term wholeness. We can start by looking at certain entities, such as apples, bodies, and planets. In that way it will get easier to grasp. Think about it like this: An apple is one whole apple, a body is one whole body, and a planet is one whole planet. Plain and simple, no hidden traps.

But then we must recognize that these examples describe single entities out of groups of many entities. There are many apples, many bodies, and many planets. However, to seek the truth of reality, we must leave the world of entities and imagine another kind of wholeness—namely, reality as one whole. One whole without a boundary. It is hard to grasp, but we cannot say that there is no such infinite wholeness. It is absolutely logical. The one whole must be one; it cannot be two. Can you picture it before you? Well, I think that you cannot. It is impossible from our point of view. We cannot both be the whole and see the whole. Not from a distance. Only from within. Only by being it.

We can try a simile advised by the great Swami Vivekananda. He suggested that we picture a robe that stretches endlessly. We then follow the robe before our mind's eye as far as we can. And from there we do it again, and again. Pretty soon, we tire from the exercise. But the robe does not tire. It continues endlessly. Is it ungraspable, or is it logical? If you ask me, I say it is logical. Endlessness is logical, if even hard to grasp.

But wholeness, which is similar to oneness, is not only dry logic, it appeals to our emotional senses too.

It is present in poetry and songs, in literature, politics, religion, and our own personal longing.

Alexander Dumas (*The Three Musketeers*) said, 'All for one and one for all.'

Winston Churchill said, 'United we stand. Divided we fall.'

Plato pointed out that we seek unity by necessity.

Bob Marley sang about 'One Love'.

Liverpool fans never walk alone.

We can all add our favourites to the list. It is a given—we long for unity; we want to agree; we want to get it all together. We want to find the way back home. The examples above are directed towards certain groups and certain issues, but according to the infinity principle, it is a general truth. The whole is one, and we are all part of it. Differentiation has value amongst personal interactions, but it dissolves in the face of oneness.

And the verse in 'Ramayana' continues: 'What has come out of the whole is also whole,' and 'When the whole is taken out of the whole, the whole still remains whole.' First we must ask, how can anything come out of the whole? Where can it go? The logical answer is that it is technically impossible. Still, we must try to understand it.

Let us join sides with science for a while and ask the laws of thermodynamics. The first law of thermodynamics says that energy can neither be created nor destroyed, which means that energy can only be transformed, which then also is constantly happening. Energy is one; it permeates everything that we know and everything we don't know, including dark matter and dark energy. The sum total of energy is one mass/unit/phenomenon, (whatever we choose to call it), that is constantly rearranging itself.

In other words, the one and the many are the same. It is hard to grasp, but we are getting closer, and we do refine our question as the computer in *The Hitchhikers Guide to the Galaxy*[23] prompted us to do. Oneness in itself is uncomplicated, and if it was all that there was, we would have had no problem. But the infinite whole is not alone. We are here. And that is just as undoubtedly true as infinity itself.

So we are like the cat that chases its own tail, surely a sight for sore eyes. The cat gets intrigued by its own tail and tries to catch it. As the tail keeps slipping away, it creates a hilarious spectacle. That is us, existential seekers; we are both the chaser and the chased.

And we are Hamlet anxiously asking, 'To be or not to be'[24], not realizing that the answer is to be *and* not to be.

Furthermore, we keep asking what came first, the hen or the egg, whilst the answer is that both have always been. Both being part of *one* eternally shifting energy. Even the Bible points out that we are in this world but not of this world, which is yet another clue. We are both sides; the two are one. So, can we have our cake and eat it too? Well, we not only can, we already do. I am pulling your leg here, but I cannot stop myself. We are stuck in an unsolvable riddle, yet we must try to solve it.

Chapter 7
THE INSIGHT

In which an ordinary day becomes extraordinary.

I have already mentioned that the aim of this book is to explain the nature of reality. I have also said that the idea that funds the reasoning, and which I have come to call the infinity principle, appeared before me as a sudden and unexpected epiphany. That don't mean that I had not pondered existential issues before. It is rather the contrary; I have been intrigued by the enigma behind our 'normal' worldview for as long as I can recall. But still, I was unprepared for this sudden answer. It may not seem very special when told back this way, but it was to me, and it is to this day. At the time that it happened my jaw dropped. I was flabbergasted. I could not believe it. At the same time I could not avoid believing it.

It took place on an early afternoon in a secluded forest house where my wife and I lived at the time. I had been studying throughout the morning and I needed a break. So I sat down on my meditation mat to quiet my thinking mind for a while. I assumed meditation pose: legs crossed, back straight, nostril breathing, expectations off, and turmoil down, allowing quietness, just as so many times before. It all went well, and I did nothing. And suddenly, as out of nowhere, an unprecedented vision appeared before me.

It is actually very difficult to describe. There were no outspoken details. But immediately I recognized that this was something that I had not encountered before. It was wordless as it happened, if it even is possible to conceive of such a notion. It was a sudden comprehension in which I, to my surprise, clearly saw that infinity is infinite. It was almost as if someone had said, 'Hey, friend, look here: it is infinite.' I did not hear these words; I just try to tell the experience. In the moment it was absolutely clear, absolutely sans of doubt. And there was more; in some strange way I sensed that all my questions had answers. Not that I had addressed any certain questions, but at the same time they were all answered. It was a bit like the *Hitchhikers Guide to the Galaxy* again. I had the answers, but I did not know the questions. But if I am forced to put words to it, I would say that I always had been disturbed by the paradoxes that keep popping up in the face of any sincere truth seeker. And here, in this moment, the paradoxes smoothly evened out. They had their role to play, but they were part of one self-evident wholeness. And it was just as it should be.

Another important thing was the total absence of doubt. Doubt has been a constant companion in my life. I have doubted myself and the world. I have felt that I had to explain myself and had done so through countless hours of inner dialogue. I have felt an urge to explain the shortcomings of the world. I still do, as it seems, writing this. But there is no doubt about the overruling purpose anymore. The infinity principle works beyond doubt. Reality is infinite, and therein lies its promise of constant bliss.

This was 2019, and six years have passed, but it is still just as clear in my mind. It amazingly reminds me of the witty words of Walt Whitman when he said, 'The truth is very simple. If it was complicated everyone would understand it.' I loved that quote the first time I heard it, and now it matches my own experience perfectly.

I had, as so many of us do, kept looking for a better conclusion in an ever-escaping distance, looking over yonder for a truth that suddenly showed up right before me. As the message kept dawning upon me, I couldn't help wondering why I had not heard about it before. It was so profound yet so simple. But then I realized that I had heard ideas like this before, just that the full message had not clicked within me until now. Having said that, I must also say that I still find the recognition of infinity's significance surprisingly underrepresented amongst existential debate, being the obvious clue to our great mysteries as it is. It is actually more than a clue. It is nothing less than the master key to an intelligible understanding of reality.

In the next chapter I will present the full idea from top down. I will guide you to the end of the rainbow and reveal the pot of gold that awaits us.

Chapter 8

TIP

*In which the full message of the infinity
principle gets described.*

In the last chapter I described the insight that completely
changed my understanding of the world. It came as a
sudden and unexpected revelation and took me by
surprise. The insight was free of thought, which is to say
that I did not think it in any deliberate way. Yet in the
moment I was aware beyond all doubt that it revealed
something accurate. In other words, I believed it, which I
still do. I had realized a truth, and it was quite profound.
Reality was infinite; it was obvious, and it explained
the lot.

But in the coming days I often had to say to myself,
'Hey, wait a minute, how can infinity explain the lot?'
Questions mounted, and I had some thinking to do. In
this process, my great advantage was the insight itself.
Whenever my mind slipped into doubt, which it did on
numerous occasions, I could still revisit that moment of
doubtlessness. And again and again it told me that reality

at its core is comprehensible, that it could be explained in an understandable way. I have subtitled this book *Answering the Mystery of Oneness,* because infinity reveals *oneness* as an impeccable truth. But what might be even more interesting is that it also reveals an intrinsic force that holds an unchallenged perpetual positive charge. That is a mouthful, I know, but I hope you bear with me as I now will try to put words to this vision.

In the first chapter I presented a concise version of the whole idea. Let us read it again before we get into explaining it.

- Infinity exists, thus absolute nothingness does not exist.
- Absolute nothingness does not exist, thus absolute equilibrium neither exists.
- Absolute equilibrium does not exist, thus one force is stronger.
- One force is stronger, thus that force is positive.

The whole idea starts with recognizing that infinity is infinite. All the following steps can be traced back to this one single fact. Infinity is certain. That is not a small thing to realize. When reality is verily scrutinized, we find that very few things are undoubtedly certain. But infinity is. Infinity is not an illusion, and it is not a subject to opinion. We need not fret that we are mistaken. There will be no, 'Sorry, infinity is not infinite anymore, reality ends here.' Thus, we can confidently proclaim infinity as being the unchangeable ground condition of reality.

Philosopher Frederic Nietzsche said, 'There are no

facts, only interpretations,' but he was wrong, at least in an absolute sense.

His statement is true as seen from the personal perspective, but it is not true as seen from the impersonal perspective. Infinity is not an interpretation; it is a fact. So this is our platform and safe haven to return to in moments of doubt.

Now let us see what follows from that.

The first step down the ladder tells us that nothingness does *not* exist. In fact, nothingness is impossible. Such statement may appear as controversial, but it is actually the second undoubtable truth about reality according to the infinity principle. It follows directly from the fact that infinity exists. Something cannot come out of nothing, and as infinity here is referred to as a something, a something that is present everywhere, it proves that nothingness cannot be. But nothingness is often debated. It is asked what it looks like, what it does, where it starts, and where it stops. The infinity principle ends that discussion by firmly stating that nothingness in an absolute sense is impossible.

It should be self-evident, but let us give it a thorough examination so that there will be no remaining doubt about this crucial part of our story. It is of course true that we experience some sort of nothingness in our personal lives and in everyday situations. But that is not the same kind of nothingness as the one we that talk about here. We do not talk about the nothing as in an empty bank account or an unfurnished room. Nor do we talk about the dark emptiness of space or a mind void of ideas. We are talking about an absolute nothingness where there is neither darkness nor light, up nor down, here nor there. There is no God, and there is no not-God. There is no infinity. There is just nothing, in fact, there is not even nothing. It may seem dreadful, and it may seem a relief, but it is neither. If this kind of nothingness had been real, we had not known about it since no one had been there. The thought of nothingness might seem scary, but there is no need for fear. On the contrary, we are absolutely safe. Infinity is our safeguard as it undoubtedly proves that nothingness is impossible. Infinity is real, and nothingness is not real.

Absolute nothingness cannot even be imagined. We cannot think it because thinking requires a thinker, and when there is a thinker, there is not nothingness. We might try to claim that nothingness could have occurred at some point in space or time. But that is also impossible. That would not have been nothingness in an absolute sense. If nothingness had been at some point, then it had always been, since somethingness cannot come out of nothingness. *If* something had come out of nothing, then the nothing had not been a nothing. It had been that which the something came out of. It had been the first mother. It had been the womb of creation. Some of us have called it God. But whatever name we gave it, it had been an origin, something that could be pointed to. And an origin, a mother, or any causing effect is not a nothing. Proper nothingness had been the end of the story; in fact, there had been no stories to begin with. And one thing that we know for certain is that there are stories, which proves that something exists. It is proven by our very existence.

The absence of nothingness is an essential insight

in an existential inquiry, and I cannot stop myself from stressing it. Let us appoint an imaginary scientist to prove the existence of nothingness. It would not help how intricate a calculation the scientist could produce; it would inevitably fail. The calculation itself would cause the calculation's downfall as a calculation is a something. Or let us assign the same scientist to construct a doomsday machine destined to terminate everything. If he succeeded, everything would blow up, the scientist included. Then all that would remain would be a black, empty void. But it would still not be nothingness. It would be a caused effect; it would have a history, and no doomsday machine in the world can change that.

Furthermore, and this will sound strange, in our minds we can erase everything except infinity. As a thought-experiment we can take away both mind and matter, we can even erase eternity, which is to say that we can erase time (hypothetically, that is). But infinity would still do all right. It would be unaffected as such, and it would still be real. We cannot erase infinity, not even thought-wise, because, again, it requires a thinker. And we know that there is a thinker, namely ourselves, which proves that infinity is real, and which at the same time proves that we are real. Nothingness, on the other hand, can for the same reasons never be real, not even hypothetically.

And then it is time for the next step. Here we must draw the somewhat strange conclusion that just as nothingness is impossible, so is an absolute equilibrium. This was actually the hardest part to capture when I started to verbalize the wordless revelation of the infinity principle.

I was certain that infinity was unchanging in itself. And unchangingness ought to equal absolute balance. In other words, an absolute equilibrium. But then I realized that in a state of absolute equilibrium, nothing happens. And that is the same as nothingness. So this was a tough nut to crack. I knew that reality was changeless at its core, but I also knew that there were change. I encountered the classical existential enigma face on. At what point did the unchanging perfectly harmonized infiniteness split up and produce imbalance? I was certain that infinity was real, and I was certain that existence was real, and thus I could not escape the fact that both these qualities were real. And then it seemed as reality was in a state of infinite imbalance. Now that may seem rather realistic at a first glance since we tend to think of reality as oscillating between equally strong negative and positive forces. But the more I pondered the infinity principle, I found that it does not. The oscillation is going on, no doubt, but only in the personal realm, only within the limits of time. If positivity and negativity had been equally strong on a permanent basis, then they had eventually equalled out and ended up in perfect balance, a perfect balance that had been the same as a permanent standstill, a permanent standstill that had been the same as nothingness, a nothingness that is impossible.

Let me give you some more clues here. Let us consider the expression 'perfect peace'. Perfect peace means that nothing disturbs the peace. But at the same time it means that nothing neither creates the peace. We can all note within ourselves that peace is not merely the absence of disturbance; it is the presence of something. We do not experience emptiness when we are peaceful, on the contrary, we experience fullness. There is an active energy involved. It is subtle, yes, but it is not dead. Something is there, some vibrant energy. The same thing can be said about harmony. Harmony is not only the absence of disharmony. It is a heightened state in itself. It contains energy. It requires some sort of beingness. Some sort of momentum. So, what is this inbuilt momentum that we experience as energy within peace and harmony? I call it the positive force. You maybe call it bliss or serenity. There may be other and better names for it. But the name is not of the essence, what is of the essence is that if everything was taken away and infinity were left all alone, it had not been peaceful as in dead and empty. It would have an intrinsic force. Either that, or it had been nothingness, and nothingness, as we know by now, cannot be. And thus we must conclude that reality is out of balance, tilted, skewed, inclined towards a perpetual continuation. One force is stronger, or it had eventually lost momentum and faded out. The pendulum had come to a halt. In other words, one side, one party, one force, one ground energy, whatever name we give it, dominates perpetually. If it had not, then there had been nothing at all.

Maybe we should stop for a moment here and recognize that unchangingness belongs to the impersonal side. The personal side is a whole other story. And here we see the big difference between the two. The impersonal side is unchanging. The personal side on the other hand, is in constant flux, oscillating between positive and negative forces, without ever reaching full contentment. Such is the nature of the personal side. Where the impersonal side is steady, the personal side is a myriad of ever-changing details. We will discuss the nature of details in the latter part of this book, but for now we keep concentrating on understanding the ground-conditions of the impersonal side of reality.

And so, we have reached the last step of the ladder which tells us that because one force is perpetually stronger, that force must be positive. Now, why must it be positive? Could it not have been negative, or at least neutral? Well, it could definitely not have been neutral. A perpetually neutral force would be the same as nothingness. But we could call it negative and presume that negativity were the stronger force. If so, positivity would play the part of the mirroring factor. We would then have promoted heartlessness, we would have celebrated selfish despots, we had said, 'I hate it', when we felt attraction towards something. We had wanted things to go wrong. It is thinkable. But here we must note that it had not changed our reasoning as such. We had traded the term positivity for negativity, but we had still been attracted to the one strongest force. If negativity had been the stronger force, then negativity had been our ideal, and then negativity had been considered positive.

There are also other reasons to call the one strongest force positive. The term positive can be used in two ways. It can be used as in giving, loving, joyful. But it can also be used as in being active. For instance, a test result may tell us that we have some sort of virus. We call that result positive, not positive as in the sense of being a good thing but in the sense of being confirmed. As in being active. And that is a rather precise description of reality; it is active, it is positive, it is confirmed. So reality is positive in both ways, both as being giving, loving, and joyous and also as in being active, as in having a purpose, as in being confirmed. We can have a bad day and want to destroy things, but we do it to gain something, we seek a positive outcome. The term positive equals being sought after. On a personal level we are always seeking a positive outcome. This is an inescapable fact. It is naturally obvious, and as already has been emphasized, obviousness is a strong indicator when it comes to seeking truth.

And there is more. All our major thought traditions teach that reality is loving at its core. Religions may display negative and unloving activities, but they ultimately describe God as loving and forgiving. Another example is Plato's idea of an intrinsic good, which points in the same direction. Or take movies and novels, even the dystopic ones convey some sort of hope in the end. A film or novel without some sort of hero is downright impossible, which then again proves that a positive outcome always is expected in the far end somehow.

Actually, we must not ask anyone else about this; we know it ourselves, as with the example about harmony. We want disharmony to go away. But we do not seek indifference. We seek a heightened state of being, we seek an improved place. When we look within ourselves, or at ourselves, it is plain to see that being loved, and to be loving, is our foremost desired goal. If we had only one option, we would choose love over mistrust. It is as certain as certain can be. And it tells us that it is not only the impersonal side of reality that is charged by a positive force but also equally true for the personal side.

Life and existence is loving at its core. We experience ups and downs, but we can confidently trust that the positive force ultimately prevails. There ain't no cure for love, as *Leonard Cohen*[25] says in his song of the same title. At least not for unconditional love. And not only because it seems like a nice thing, but because it cannot be any other way. That is the essence of the message given by the infinity principle.

Chapter 9

EXPERIENCING

In which we seek the intermedia between the two realms.

We have focused on explaining the impersonal side of reality, and it has become time to turn our attention towards its personal side. Where the impersonal side is all about abstract phenomena and fundamental, unchanging truths, the personal side is quite its opposite. Before we start decipher the differences, let us remember that the unchanging truths are not so much about us as people. If we were not here, if there were no planets or stars, if there was no universe at all, the unchanging truths would still be true. The impersonal side of reality would in itself be the same even without a material world. But as we all know, there is a material world. And we are part of it. So what do you say? Shall we try to understand how it's put together?

Let us start by sorting the rather deceptive, yet surprisingly often posed question—namely, if there is a material world at all. Why would I call it deceptive? Well, on an everyday basis we experience the physical world as tangible and solid, but amongst deep investigators of reality we often hear that the world is an illusion.

And even scientific researchers, when using microscopes to penetrate the world of matter, finds that matter actually dissolves into tinier and tinier components, finally ending up in almost nothing. It is not absolutely nothing; there is still measurable activity of sorts, there is still a temperature, but solid matter as we experience it dissolves into an ever-changing spacious void. And this phenomenon seems to be equally true when we turn our attention to the macro-cosmos. In the far-far end, the universe again seems to dissolve into a nothingness of sorts, drifting further and further apart, eventually turning into a void. Or if it turns back into itself, disappearing into singularities. There are different scientific theories. But even if none of these theories ends up in an absolute nothing, they do challenge our comprehension of a solid material world. This is noteworthy because it indicates a continuation beyond material physics, given by scientific physics itself.

There are of course even stranger theories. One idea suggests an indefinite number of universes where our own universe even repeats itself and where we are the same people under the same circumstances but making other choices. To me, that is a rather meaningless thought. But our attempts to explain reality in terms of physical matter is interesting, not only because of its fascinating multitude, but maybe even more because it points to a somethingness beyond matter. It seems unavoidable that there is a metaphysical side to it, no matter how strongly physicalists try to find other explanations. In the context of the infinity principle, we use infinity itself as reference, because even if infinity is not a thing, but 'merely' a principle, it is indestructible and it can confidently be relied upon. It tells us that something always remains, and thereby it also explains our compulsion to ask what is going on beyond the apparent world. Infinity proves that the physical world of matter only is a restricted part of the whole, and that reality has other sides to it.

Historically, there has been many attempts to explain how reality is constituted. Here are some examples. Thomas Aquinas 1225—1274 was an early advocate for connecting faith with logical reasoning. Aquinas came out of Christian belief which owes its understanding to Jesus of Nazareth whom among other things said, 'I and my Father is one', a statement that points out personality on one hand and impersonality on the other. Before Jesus we have the old testimony where God appears in front of Moses in the form of a burning bush. When Moses asks God, 'Who are you?', God replies, 'I am that I am.' This sounds rather cryptic, but it makes sense in the light of the infinity principle. Infinity also 'is that it is'.

A similar oddity was given by the Buddha when he was still sitting beneath the bodhi tree soon after his enlightenment. He was asked who he was, and he answered, 'I am the Buddha', which literally means 'I am the enlightened.' And when he was asked for proof, he tapped on the ground and said, 'The earth is my witness.' If you ask me, he thereby points to the natural obviosity that reality is what it is.

Still, personal statements, just as religious beliefs, especially those with an initial creating God involved, can be logically doubted. This dilemma led the seventeenth-century philosopher Descartes to commit thought-experiments where he deliberately tried to erase all that could be doubted. This is from where his famous quote, 'I think, therefore I am', is taken. Descartes reasoned that even if reality were illusionary, if it was just a dream, or even worse, if his mind were controlled by a demon that tricked him to see a world that did not exist, he could still not erase the fact that he thought about it.

Swami Sarvapriyananda[26] has said in one of his many brilliant YouTube lectures, 'The fact that everything can be doubted proves without a doubt that there is a doubter.' Which points out that doubtlessly there is a personal self who 'experiences' reality. Yet, we are tempted by ideas of deception. The Descartes demon reappears in the movie *The Matrix*, where humanity is unknowingly trapped within a simulated reality. The discussion about what is real or not is per definition confusing, but at least one certain truth can be drawn—namely, that there is a personal self. Something is being experienced, and someone does the experiencing. It is difficult to give it a precise description, but we cannot deny that it exists.

There are other attempts to try to explain this enigma. The Buddhists claim, through the concept of Sunyata, that there are no objects. They go on to say that there is no self, that we are left with nothing but experience alone. A full understanding of this is said to lead to Nirvana. Buddha himself lived twenty-five hundred years ago, long before Jesus, Thomas of Aquinas, or Descartes; he sprang out of the Vedic tradition, which of course is even more ancient. Buddha awakened and became liberated from the wheel of Samsara. This was a personal experience out of which Buddhism evolved.

Another Vedic example that was practiced long before the Buddha is the method of Tantra. This is a powerful discipline that merges the two fundamental principles, *Shiva* and *Shakti*, into one— Shiva as the supporting root principle, and Shakti as the creative force.

Obviously, our longing to find the connection between the impersonal and personal realms has followed humankind for as long as we know. But if you think these ancient examples to be vague and esoteric, unsuited for an age of material physics perhaps, then you should remember that some of our most acclaimed scientists have taken great interest in the Vedas. Robert Oppenheimer, the man with the bomb, for instance, knew Sanskrit and studied the Vedas. When overlooking the first atomic explosion, he famously paraphrased a verse taken from the Bhagavad Gita, 'Now I have become Death, the Destroyer of Worlds.'

Another prominent example is Erwin Schrodinger. Schrodinger received the Nobel Prize in physics in 1933 due to his work in quantum mechanics where the Schrodinger equation was, and is, an important part. In some of his speeches, he half humorously mentions what he calls 'Schrodinger's second equation', namely *Atman equals Brahman*. This is originally a Vedic idea where Brahman represents infinite oneness, and Atman represents the personal self, and thus points out that the two are one. There are other intriguing examples on this subject. Meister Eckhart, who was an acclaimed German theological philosopher in the thirteenth century, said, *'The eye through which I see God is the same eye through which God sees me; my eye and God's eye are one eye, one seeing, one knowing, one love.'* Which says that the viewer and the viewed are one and the same. And not only that, but that it is loving too.

And then we revisit *The Hitchhikers Guide to the Galaxy*[27], where two young earthlings ask the question regarding life, the universe, and everything. The answering supercomputer says that they do not understand his answer because they do not understand the question. Well, we have at least defined the question by now; how can the two be one, and how can the one be two?

This is the crucial threshold that every existential inquiry sooner or later stumbles upon. This is the crossroad where the two realms meet. This is where we must try to intelligibly connect the two sides, physics/metaphysics, multitude/oneness, changing/unchanging, personal/impersonal. All the examples above talks about a personal versus an impersonal realm. On one hand, there is an unescapable great truth, and on the other, there is a 'person' who 'experiences' it. The difficulty is twofold: first we must identify the personal self, and then we must locate the meeting point between the two different realms. There is no obvious boarder station to be found. There is no direct connection point. I named this chapter Experiencing for a specific reason. I suggest experiencing to be the interface between the physical and metaphysical realms.

Experiencing, as such, is an ability that is so natural to us that we never think twice about it. But to be sure, it is an ability. It is something that we do. Experiencing, at least as we know it, takes place within organic life. It is hard to imagine how planets, stars, or other inanimate entities experience their existence. Still, we cannot deny that they too are players in the personal realm. They too are changing, that much is certain, even if we cannot describe their point of view.

Can we define the term experiencing? The best-suited descriptions I found so far suggest 'involvement', or 'meeting or feeling something first-hand'. Feelings seems to play a significant part. But feelings are deceptive. It is often said that our feelings don't lie, but at the same time, feelings are momentary and fleeting, and they cannot be trusted to lead us right at all times. The same can be said about all our senses. Not even our instincts can always be trusted. Besides and above these parameters, we have our intelligible cognition, our ability to understand things. All in all, these interacting abilities make up our sense of experiencing the world. And as I have said before, it seems that *understanding* is the prime governor that surpasses all the other faculties.

Let us note another thing, (and this is actually where the infinity principle explains why there is suffering in the world). There must be different options for experience to even occur. There must be more and less desired outcomes. This is necessary. If everything were unchangingly the same, absolutely neutral, for example, then experiencing would not occur. Even if everything was constantly positive, experiencing would have lost its value. We would not have noticed any differences. If reality was 100 percent good, experiencing would be superfluous. And this actually explains why there is evil in the world. Evil, suffering, and misfortune are the necessary mirroring factors for experience to arise at all. Now, evil is an extreme, and we do not want extremes, we want to be balanced. But we have found the mechanics behind why evil, misfortune, and suffering occurs in the first place.

Experiencing requires counterparts. There must be a mile to walk. That is not a cliché; it is the way that it is. It is the very nature of the personal side, at least to us, the members of organic life. What about planets and stars? Does a planet that is hit by a meteor suffer? Does a star grieve coming to its end? We don't know. But we do know that without having alternative options, we would not experience good over bad.

Neil Young, in his song 'Nothing Is Perfect',[28] says: 'Nothing is perfect in God's perfect plan, just look in the shadows to see. He only gave us the good sides so we understand what life without him would be.'

The infinity principle does not involve a god figure, but it can still agree with Neil Young here. The notion of experiencing has undeniable significance when we try to understand reality as a whole. Thus, experiencing can be seen as an interface between the two realms. Reality as seen from the impersonal perspective is 100 percent positive. But without the experienced differences of the personal realm, we'd have no way to know. At least not in the way we normally mean when saying 'to know'.

Chapter 10

TIME

Deeper into the nature of experiencing.

We have decided to use experiencing as the connecting interface between the two sides. Now we must dive deeper into the nature of the personal realm.

Our next step is the intimate relation between experiencing and time. We have concluded that experiencing is dependent on differences, but what is needed for differences to occur? Well, one necessary component is *time*. It is very hard to imagine differences without time being involved. Someone has said that *if there were no time, then everything would have happened at once.* A somewhat incomprehensible thought, still it carries some sort of truth. There must be a distance between two different points of view. And distances require time intervals. If there were no time interval between two different occurrences, it would be impossible to separate them. It would seem as if they were one and the same. There had been no way to make a distinction. Experiencing as we know it requires time.

The time issue has been discussed by scientists and philosophers for millennia. It is one of our great mysteries. And it is an ongoing project to this day. Just consider superposition and entanglement as described by quantum physics. Here interactions happen simultaneously over distances without time delay.

I do not pretend that I will be the first to intelligibly explain time. But as I find myself in good company amongst non-understanders, I dare to venture on a rather wild excursion concerning this delicate matter.

But before I do, let us have a short résumé of scientific conclusions about time and causation. I must warn you that we will be looking at physics on the Nobel Laureate level. Some of it will appear rather incomprehensible, even to the experts. My intention here is not to try to explain it in detail; for that you will need to seek elsewhere. But it is important to notify some of the conclusions and findings that science has brought up, so that we can use it to understand reality as a whole. So let us take a quick look at some of the important thinkers down the line of modern thinking.

- Isaac Newton (1642–1727) is famous for getting a falling apple in the head, which led him to understand the law-bound motions of the universe. Whether the apple story is true or not, does not matter, Newton was undoubtedly an extraordinary thinker whose understanding about how gravity stirs the stars, thereby affects every single entity in the known universe, is fundamental knowledge to this day. But concerning the time issue, Newton had a rather primitive narration. He considered time to be absolute and unchanging regardless of how it was measured. To Newton, time was independent to its observer. (This was before Albert Einstein, who said that the rate of time is dependent on the relation between moving objects and thereby affected by the observer's point of view.)

- People like us (then–now). Let us note that on an everyday basis, we ordinary people, people like us, agree with Newton's interpretation of time. To us, time is a very straightforward matter. We do know that we must adjust our clocks when we cross over into other time zones, but apart from that, time seems coherent and identical to us all. Yesterday is gone, tomorrow is yet to come, and we are in between in the everyday moment.

- Arthur Eddington (1882–1944), professor at Cambridge, coined the well-known expression 'The arrow of time,' which highlights that time is pointed in one direction only. It is a rather straightforward description on how people like us perceive time in the macroscopic world. But the arrow of time concept has a deeper layer as it addresses the fact that the microscopic world behaves differently. By *macroscopic*, we mean the large world as we see it from an everyday physical viewpoint. This is where time constantly moves in a forward direction. The *microscopic* world, the world of atoms and particles, on the other hand, seems capable of other solutions.

More about that later. Arthur Eddington was a remarkable scientist, and he is a good example of highly acclaimed physicists who extend their reasoning into the metaphysical sphere[29]. He is also remembered as being the first initiated scientist outside Germany who understood, and helped develop, the greatness of the young Albert Einstein and the remarkable theories brought forward by the relativity principle.

- Albert Einstein (1879–1955) needs no further introduction. He introduced space-time, which means that when Newton and people like us see the world as three-dimensional, Einstein combined it with time into a four-dimensional interrelated continuum. He also made clear that there is no absolute fixed time, and that time is dependent on the conditions of the entity that relates to it.

There are three very intriguing components to note here, at least as far as I am able to understand it. First, gravity slows down time. Time is affected by gravitational objects. When light bends around a planet, for instance, it is not that it travels slower in the inner curve where the distance is shorter, it is time that slows down. The light in itself has constant, uninterrupted speed (in vacuum, that is). Secondly, the passage of time depends on the speed of the entity that relates to it, which means that something that travels fast 'ages slower' than something that doesn't. These are undisputed facts according to the relative principle. Thirdly, and which stunningly enough seems to have been one of Albert Einstein's very early insights: time stands still at the speed of light. Rather mind-blowing, to say the least.

- Max Planck (1858–1947) discovered quantum physics, which rendered him the Nobel Prize in Physics in 1918. Furthermore, he proposed what now is called the Planck units. That is a coherent table of measurements at the atomic level. They include the concept of Planck length, which is accepted as our smallest measurable unit. It has been described by Professor Alden Mead of the university of Minnesota, saying, 'It is impossible, using the known laws of quantum mechanics and the known behaviour of gravity, to determine a position to a precision smaller than the Planck length.'

And then we have Planck time, the shortest possible measurement of time, according to this viewpoint. But then again, this seems contradictory to me; photons, massless particles of light, need Planck time to travel Planck lengths, which then would say that photons are even smaller than Planck units. It sounds contradictory, but then again, it is also said that nothing with mass can travel at the speed of light. Thus, a photon is a different side of physical reality altogether. And again, as Albert Einstein said, time stands still at the speed of light. Yes, you hear for yourself—I do not grasp it fully. I can only recommend anyone who is interested to further examine the details. I know one thing. Infinity is still unaffected.

- In the EPR Paper (1935), the three scientists (Einstein, Nathan Rosen, and Boris Podolsky) wrote this now famous paper to show that the theories of quantum mechanics were wrong, or at least incomplete. Einstein could not believe in what he famously called *spukhafte fernwirkung* (spooky action at a distance). Thus, he rejected the idea that information could change position instantaneously and thereby surpass the speed of light.
- Niels Bohr (1885–1962) studied atoms and quantum physics. In 1922 he received a Nobel Prize for his work. He was the head of the so-called Copenhagen Project, where Werner Heisenberg, Max Born, and a few more prominent scientists also took part. This lot were highly responsible for the development of quantum physics. Out of their work sprang the theories of entanglement and the uncertainty principle. Entanglement, then, says that certain particles have the ability to pass information instantaneously over distances, and that time as we know it is out of play. Which then was what Einstein, Rosen, and Podolsky rejected. The uncertainty principle proposes that it is impossible to simultaneously measure both the speed and the position of a particle in a correct way because the measuring itself alters the result. And this phenomenon is said to occur whether there is an observer or not. Which then seems to mean that the outcome of an action

is undetermined until it, for some reason, gets determined.

- John Stewart Bell (1928–90) was an Irish scientist who challenged the EPR Paper and in 1964 presented Bell's theorem, which suggested that the debated idea of *entanglement* indeed was correct. Alain Aspect, John Clauser, and Anton Zeilinger tested John Bell's ideas independently through different experiments. In 2022 the three shared the Nobel Prize in Physics for proving that John Bell was right. Thus, we can conclude that the physical sides of reality seen by *people like us* act in strange ways and that our concept of time is only partly true.

With this information taken into account, it is clear that we don't have a complete understanding of *time*. And when contemplating the first law of thermodynamics it leaves the explanation even more open-ended. The first law of thermodynamics says that energy can neither be created nor destroyed. If this is true, then there is never any new energy. There is only one permanent amount of energy that is constantly being transformed into new shapes and new motions. Furthermore, this one energy is unchangingly present all the time in every part of our universe in the forms of physical matter, dark matter, and dark energy.

Now, let us allow ourselves to elaborate freely here. Let us consider planet Earth. It seems certain that it was here yesterday. But in a timewise sense, yesterday is gone. Clearly, it remains in our memories, but we cannot go back there. And in that sense it does not really exist anymore. And then we can ask ourselves, is Earth still here yesterday? It sounds like a crazy question, but I mean it seriously. We normally think that Earth is present even in the past, just that we cannot go there. But if we thoroughly scrutinize the first law of thermodynamics, it seems that it is not so. According to the law of thermodynamics, the law of conservation, all energy is constantly consumed in an ever-ongoing transformation into new forms and new motions. Some of it seems to happen fast, and some of it seems to happen slow, but nevertheless, it all takes place in the same present moment. And if all energy is occupied by making up the present moment, what energy makes up Earth yesterday?

This question leads to a radical proposal. When contemplated freely, the movement of time disappears. Past, present, and future all happens in the now. That is not how we experience it, but can it be in any other way? The past does not happen anymore, the future has not happened yet, so what remains is the now, the present moment. When I started to think about this I realized that I had always seen the future as an already existing room that awaited me to enter. As if the universe was already there, so to speak. But then I thought, *If the future is already there, readymade in advance, whose future would that be? Would it be mine or would it be yours?* This led me to realize that everything happens in the now. It simply cannot be in any other way. We can measure time in different ways, but infinity, eternity, and the whole spectacle of existence happens right now. The arrow of time is pointed, but it never escapes the now.

We often use expressions as 'since time began' and 'until the end of time'. But are there really such things as beginnings and ends? According to the infinity principle there is not, at least not in an ultimate sense.

Let us compare time to eternity and start by placing infinity, eternity, and time in their right order. As has already been stated, infinity would be real even without eternity whilst eternity had not been real without infinity. And the same idea applies in a next step too. Eternity had been real without time, but time had not been real without eternity. Now, what insights might we draw from this? Well, eternity is of course eternal, and I would say that time is too. And furthermore, it must also be true for the chain of causation. And right here we come across another way to illumine the interface between the unchanging and the changing, between the impersonal and the personal. Eternity belongs to the impersonal realm, whilst time belongs to the personal realm. Eternity is not an active player in itself. It is rather a state of potentiality that enables time to occur. And in a similar way, time is the media that enables experience to occur. This reasoning seems to suggest that infinity and eternity are fundamental properties whilst time and experience are not. Infinity and eternity had been all right even without time or experiencing, whilst time and experiencing could not have been without infinity and eternity.

All right, this is a wild excursion, just as I promised. So, everything happens in the now. And let us be absolutely clear about that—*there is only one now*. There are not different nows. Everything that happens, happens in this same now. It is incomprehensible yet at the same time logical. Obviously, the impersonal side of reality happens in the now. Think about it. Being infinite and eternal—where can that be if not here and now? And then we have the personal side. This too happens in one ever revolving now.

Personally, I picture it as a wave, an ever-rolling, all-encompassing wave. Unchanging at essence, yet in a state of progress. Moving in the direction of the *time arrow*. Moving and not moving at the same time. I do not see it as a fixed position but rather as a room, a motion, a space. Yes I know, it is a crazy idea, and I can only recommend you paint your own picture. But in whatever way we picture it, we cannot escape the fact that time is now. Or that the now is *one*. It simply cannot be in any other way, whether we are able to grasp it or not.

And then lastly, let us again return to the planets, stars, and other inanimate entities. Planets and stars move through time. Our sun, for instance, had a beginning, and it will come to an end. A beginning and an end, a distance in between, a pretty precise definition of time in action. Again we see that planets and stars are players within the personal realm, and we get reminded that the changing side of reality includes enormous multitude, an insight that is both humbling and exhilarating at the same time. The moment of now is a never-ending story, and we are dancers in its endless swirl.

Chapter 11

CONSCIOUSNESS

We examine a reborn notion within the
field of existential understanding.

The infinity principle firmly describes reality as one all-encompassing whole. Its main characteristic is its infiniteness. There is nothing before or beyond infinity. Everything is included, nothing can be added, nothing can be removed. And in that sense it is unchangeable. Thus we have established an understanding for the unchanging side of reality, and we are left with trying to explain the ongoing changingness as we experience it through our sense perceptions. We have already talked about the notions of *experiencing* and *time*. Now we have another component to address, namely, *consciousness*.

For long times, especially in the western thought-tradition, consciousness has been seen as a physical process in the brain. However, in recent years we have started to see a shift in attitude. David Chalmers has coined the term *The Hard Problem of Consciousness*, which has become a common expression. It is not only due to David

Chalmers, but suddenly it has become legitimate to ask deep questions about the nature of consciousness. What we see here is not only a shift in attitude, but it is actually a shift within the scientific method as such. Science's first rule is to establish proven verifiability. But the hard problem of consciousness cannot really be treated in such way. Which is why it is called the hard problem. The word hard here refers to going beyond scientific verifiability. It has its counterpart in the easy problem of consciousness, which deals with interpreting data from measured brain-activity. This is of course also a field in progress. The hard problem, however, deals with questions such as, what is the self? What is a first-person experience? What is the true nature of consciousness in a larger scheme?

To get some historical background, let us revisit the scientists from the last chapter and start with Isaac Newton once more. Newton, as many western scientists up to the twentieth century, believed in God. And thus he believed in some sort of consciousness that exceeds our own. Because that is a given, belief in God equals believing in a metaphysical realm of some sort. Einstein, on the other hand, did not believe in God. But still he sensed some sort of order behind the physical reality. He has said that he believed in Spinoza's kind of God, which is an all-pervading God beyond religion. And Einstein was not alone. There are many examples of twentieth-century scientists who claim to be atheists but ponder some sort of scheme beyond the material world. Max Planck said the following when interviewed in 1931 by the British newspaper *The Observer*: 'I regard consciousness as fundamental. I regard matter as derivative from consciousness. We cannot get behind consciousness. Everything that we talk about, everything we regard as existing, postulates consciousness.' He clearly places consciousness before matter. It should also be noted that Max Planck was a Godly man, even if he, as he said, 'first and foremost sought intelligent thought and clear understanding'. It seems that he reconciled these two seemingly opposing worldviews. An approach that I myself find rather appealing.

When we hear that our most prominent scientists either believes in God or ponders other metaphysical ideas, it actually seems quite strange that we are so keen on putting our faith in materialistic explanations. Yes, it is easier to believe in steadfast matter, but our firsthand experience of consciousness undeniably challenges us to look further. Let us now leave western thought for a bit and see what eastern philosophy have to say about this topic.

- Daoism is considered a world religion, even though there is no god involved. It is rather a philosophical idea. Daoism refers to the Dao, which simply means the Way. Dao is an unconditional state that is prior to everything else. Everything arises out of the Dao, which also means that Dao is prior to consciousness. The Dao does not do anything. Still, it allows for everything to be done. There is nothing before it or after it, and it cannot change. Thus it has quite a few resemblances to the infinity principle, one might say.

- Shintoism has neither a central god figure nor a specifically outlined philosophy. And in that sense, it is refreshingly simplistic. There is a godly realm called Kami. Kami is pure, and consequently, Shintoism prescribes pureness in life. Kami is not explained in great detail, but there is no doubt that reality has larger extension than what the physical world gives at hand.

- Buddhism intricately talks of different layers of consciousness. From a certain point of view there are four layers of consciousness, and from another angle there are nine layers. All in all, an understanding of consciousness is recommended by Buddhism, but first and foremost to help us go beyond suffering. Nirvana is the goal, but Nirvana is not similar to consciousness; rather, it is beyond consciousness. A bit like Dao in Daoism.

- Hinduism, or the Vedic tradition, is one of the oldest recorded thought traditions in the world. Yet it includes elements that are straight-up-to-date with a modern discussion about consciousness. The Vedic narration is vast and rich, but it finds a common ground in what is called Brahman. The term Brahman simply means *the vast* and is described as reality's infinite essence. Moreover, it is attributed with a concept called *sat-chit-ananda*, where *sat* means existence or beingness, *chit* means consciousness or awareness, and *ananda* means happiness, joy, or bliss. These elements combined represents the essential nature of reality. What should also be noted here is that consciousness and mind are described as separated by the Vedas. Consciousness is impersonal, and mind is personal. Consciousness is metaphysical, whilst mind is physical. Consciousness is fundamental and mind is a derivative.

This was a very short summary of an issue that has occupied the human mind for millennia. Today it seems a circle has been fulfilled and we are back to where we were before, only now with an enhanced intellectual understanding. We now start to reconcile a connection between the physical and the metaphysical spheres in a graspable way, thereby opening up our imagination towards a greater understanding. And in the wake of this, the old term *panpsychism* has caught new attention.

The term panpsychism was first coined by an Italian philosopher in the sixteenth century, but the idea that it refers to is much older than so. We might call it the first ontological conclusion, although the matter was pondered long before the concept of ontology was even invented. By the way, the term ontology is made out of two Greek words, where *on* means existence or beingness, and *logo* means meaning or study. Thus, it is the study of the meaning of existence.

The word panpsychism is made up in the same way, where pan means *all* and psyche means *mind*, or *soul*. In other words, panpsychism suggests that consciousness is an intrinsic property of reality and that it pervades every element, be it physical or metaphysical. The opposite of panpsychism would be strict physicalism, which says that everything of importance is found within physical matter and that everything, including consciousness, emerges out of that physical matter. Yes, it is tempting to place consciousness in the brain, since it is hard to imagine consciousness without a brain involved. But then again, it is not impossible. Italian scientist Stefano Mancuso, for instance, in his book *The Revolutionary Genius of Plants* (Mancuso 2017)[30] makes a strong case that plants make conscious decisions. Yet plants do not have brains.

Physicalists remarks that consciousness disappears when we are under anaesthesia or are knocked out for other reasons. And we may ask ourselves where consciousness goes when we are unconscious. The panpsychists' answer would be that it does not go anywhere. It is there all along. Our minds shut down, but consciousness itself is unaffected. It readily awaits us as soon as our brains are safe and sound again.

Panpsychism, or varieties thereof, is common in many thought traditions. It is clearly spied amongst the old Greek philosophers; it is found within the Vedic tradition, and it is said to be a natural comprehension amongst indigenous cultures. It cannot really be called a religious worldview since it does not need an outspoken God figure. Rather, it finds God in everything. One example is the vision of the Great Spirit as suggested by Native Americans. The Great Spirit lives in everything: wind, water, mountains, plants, animals, and human beings. It can be seen as naive or wishful, but it is actually quite logical. I mean, if there is spirit at all, where would it be? If there is spirit within us, but not within water, for instance, and we drink a glass of water, at what point does the spiritless water become part of our spirit?

What about nature? I spent periods of time in the artic zone. There is not much organic life there besides polar bears, walruses, seals, and birds. There's a lot of ice. On Svalbard there are mountains. But nothing much really grows there. Can we say that such places are free of soul, free of beauty? Is it only soul-filled in our eyes? Or is soul and beauty there even when no one sees it?

According to panpsychism, spirit is within everything. The problem for the curious mind, or to phrase it academically, the epistemological problem to an existential inquiry is to find the boundaries for the personal self. In other words, who, what, and where is *the personal self* that experiences the unbound spirit, and by what sorts of limits is it held?

We have used the terms ontology and panpsychism. And we have thrown in another term constructed by Greek words, namely *epistemology*. *Episteme* means knowledge, and *logo* means meaning/study/reason. In other words, it is the study of how we know what we know. Epistemology may seem like an unnecessary discipline. Indeed, in everyday matters we do not need to understand the underlying processes that makes us know what we know. But then again, understanding the nature of consciousness is not an everyday matter. And neither is the search for the personal self. In other words, what we do here is not an everyday activity. It is an existential inquiry aimed to understand the true nature of reality. This is the role of the infinity principle.

The infinity principle certainly has epistemological significance. When we ask ourselves how we know that infinity is infinite, the answer is that we just know. That is an abstract answer, yes, but nevertheless, it cannot be falsified. It is not a theory. We cannot say that we guess that infinity is infinite. That would be ridiculous. Nor can we say that science has proven that infinity is infinite. That would also be ridiculous. Infinity is the core principle of reality and needs not be explained. We know it within. We do not need to ask anyone. It is a knowledge that we are entitled to.

The infinity principle claims certainty in its basic conclusions. Reality as seen from the impersonal side is one infinite whole. Because of its *isness* it is said to have force. Because of its *oneness* it is said to be fundamentally positive. These claims are logically confirmed.

But what about consciousness? Panpsychism says that consciousness is fundamental, and the question arises whether the infinity principle agrees. This is tricky in an epistemological sense. Does consciousness belong to the impersonal or the personal realm? Is consciousness at its core changing or unchanging? Is it an emerging property that has risen at some point and will fade away at another? Or is it an eternally intrinsic component of reality? Are Daoism and Buddhism right when they claim that there is a fundamental reality beyond consciousness? If so, is Spirit in Native American belief, or Kami in Shintoism, simply emerging properties? Max Planck said, 'We cannot get behind consciousness.' Is it just we who cannot get behind it, or is consciousness inescapable per definition? I vote for the latter.

The infinity principle does not give a straight answer here. Consciousness might be a personal emerging attribute, or it might be an impersonal intrinsic property.

Or it might be both. It will depend on what we mean by consciousness. What the infinity principle is absolutely clear about is that reality at its core is *positively charged*, and therefore it can be said to be active. If we interpret this *active charge* as conscious or not may be a matter of choice.

The topic of consciousness is fascinating, fun, and intriguing, and I could go on about it for hours. Yet it is time for closure. But before we drop the subject for the time being, let me add a couple of short notes.

- For those who wants to investigate the connection between mind, experience, and consciousness for themselves, let me suggest the following. It is an old yogic exercise, and it has two steps. It goes like this: Close your eyes and let your mind relax. When relaxed, try in your mind to locate the borderline between your consciousness and the rest of reality.

- Or try this thought exercise. Artificial Intelligence is called Artificial Intelligence and not Artificial Consciousness. Intelligence seems to be a personal attribute, an emerging timebound property that arises under certain circumstances. As such, it might very possibly be adaptable to humanmade devices. But would that be true for consciousness too?

- Lastly: If consciousness and mind are one and the same, as physicalism/emergerism proclaims, then consciousness surely is limited since our minds cannot perceive everything. But if our minds operate within consciousness, then consciousness might be fundamental. And then our minds should be able to travel within this all-pervading consciousness without restrictions. At least within its own span of time. This possibility seems plausible when a distinction between *states* of consciousness and the *nature* of consciousness is made. No matter how deep and diverse our perceptions of conscious appearances might be, there can still be levels of consciousness beyond what we can possibly perceive of. Is there a physical or nonphysical basis to consciousness? Is consciousness a fundamental property, an intrinsic part of reality, or not? I am asking you.

Chapter 12

FREE WILL

*In which we find that things don't happen for a
meaning, but that they get meaning as they happen.*

We have investigated the nature of *experiencing, time,*
and *consciousness.* All three are said to be necessary
components when trying to explain the connection
between the impersonal and the personal realm. In the
coming three chapters, including the one we're discussing,
we will look at three topics with the potential to enhance
our understanding of the personal side: free will, the
concept of God, and the meaning of life.

First is free will, the thrilling topic that engages
science, religion, and philosophy. There are numerous
arguments for and against. Some say that free will is
inevitable, some say that it is impossible. Eighteenth-
century scientist Pierre-Simone de Laplace famously
proposed an idea that has become known as *Laplace's
Demon.* He suggested that if an able intelligence knew all
the certain specifics of a certain state at a certain time,
that intelligence could correctly describe its past as well

as its future. He thereby said that everything is what it is by necessity. So no free will here.

Laplace was not the first to suggest such an idea, and he is certainly not the last. On the contrary, this remarkable idea prevails. And why remarkable? Well, it claims that the future is predetermined and that everything has to be as it has to be. But there are many ways to challenge this thought. One way would be to compare it to the theory of evolution, also known as the survival of the fittest. How can anything be called fittest in a predestined world? If evolution is predetermined, then it cannot be said to involve personal achievements. There would be no agents. In an inevitable and automatic succession no one is personally responsible for their acts. Nor can anyone, or anything, be called fittest. Everything happens as already predestined. We can then set aside every ambition to create anything at all. I think you will agree with me that it sounds rather strange. We definitely feel that we make choices and that we have the possibility, and the responsibility, to improve the future.

We can ask ourselves what would happen if there were such things as the all-knowing able intelligence that Laplace suggests in his thought-experiment. That 'intelligence' had to be outside the chain of events that it watches. And if the watcher of the all is outside the all, then the all is no longer the all. There would be the watcher and the watched. And it seems the demon would be infinite whilst the predestined world would be finite. This is called dualism in philosophical and religious debate. It suggests that there is an infinite creator on one hand and a timebound creation on the other. These two are separate; they are not one.

The infinity principle tells another story. It says that all is one and that the watcher is part of the all too. The all is watched by itself rather than being watched from the outside. The Big One, *the all*, cannot be watched from the outside; it can only be watched from within. The one itself knows everything that happens in the ever ongoing now. And Laplace's Demon is no demon after all but another word for beingness itself.

But what about free will? If free will is real, then there must be chance. Predetermination cannot be absolute.

Let us dig deeper and look at religion again. Religion addresses this issue from another viewpoint and puts emphasis on moral behaviour. God has given humans free will to be sinful or to be righteous of his or her own choices. And humans will be punished or rewarded accordingly. Such free will regulates us to do as we are told. This is a limited version of free will. Religion sometimes suggests that God already knows everything. Such an idea certainly implies predeterminism. If everything can be known in advance, then everything must be predestined, one way or another.

Alternatively, God judges every action as they occur. Which would mean that God has free will, whilst his creation does not. In such a story God is one, and the creation is a supplement. Twoness instead of oneness. But note that this is not the same twoness that the infinity principle suggests. The infinity principle only divides the one into two in order to make it comprehensible. It does not to say that the one is two. According to the infinity principle, the infinite one contains all. The all is one, but it is experienced as being two.

But either way we look at the religious explanation, God himself cannot be entirely free since he cannot stop being God. We talk more about that in the next chapter. Let us turn to philosophy and see what they have to say about free will.

Philosophy says that in order for free will to be absolutely free, it needs to operate within an unpredictable randomness where anything can happen at every given moment. Otherwise it would not be free in the absolute sense of the word. But such an idea is practically impossible to conceive of. It clashes against the timebound logic of the observable world. Another philosophical input might be that if we have free will, then we can choose to say that we have free will, but we can also choose to say that we do not have free will. And where do such arguments take us? I don't know. And then again, if we don't have free will at all, then we just say what we say, and there is nothing more to it.

English philosopher John Locke (1632–1704) suggested that it is not the will that is free but the mind. It seems to mean that the world tags along in a deterministic manner but that the personal entity can, willingly or unwillingly, alter that chain of events. That sound pretty fair to me.

German philosopher Arthur Schopenhauer (1788–1860) added, 'Man can do as he will, but not will as he will.' This quote Albert Einstein took solace in. He found it 'to mercifully mitigate the paralyzing sense of responsibility coming out of taking oneself and other people too seriously' (Einstein 2018)[31].

However, to people like us, in the stride of everyday life, it is natural to make choices. Indeed, we cannot stop ourselves from doing so. As my good friend Kenneth said, 'The only thing we cannot choose is to avoid making choices.'

But then again, to make successful choices, we must be able to control the outcome of these choices. And then free will equals control. Which is rather funny since control and freedom are usually seen as opposites.

Related to free will is destiny. There is a proverb: 'Every snowflake falls in its right place.' It suggests that everything happens as it is meant to happen and that it happens for a reason. It is an appealing thought.

In retrospect, we often say, 'It was meant to happen.' Thus, our responsibility is diminished, as Albert Einstein just noted, and then we can comfortably put our trust in a higher power. However, I was witnessing a whirling snowstorm last winter and it seemed obvious to me that the dancing snowflakes landed by chance, rather than hitting a predestined spot. Of course, the falling snowflakes were bound to land, but not in a precise location. It seemed that every action is influenced by other actions, which in turn influences new actions. Now, that is not an odd idea; on the contrary, it is the law of causality again. Or the law of karma, if you prefer the eastern variant. In either case, everything is influenced by former actions. The snowflake eventually lands at the end of its journey, influenced by fickle winds, the specifics of the terrain, and the interaction with its fellow whirling flakes. Thus we can conclude that things don't happen out of a certain predestined meaning but rather *that they get meaning as they happen.* The outcome of every event will have its meaning. Whether it is to our liking or not is another story.

But again, we must differ between the impersonal and the personal realm. Within the personal realm nothing is predetermined in an absolute sense. It is influenced by an accumulated probability that sparks new potential in the making. Like our previous description of the now, where *the wave of now* contains everything as it rolls along. Every event is then a fruit of former events, charged by a former energy. Not predestined in advance, open to choices, open to chance, driven by will, conscious or not. Every single moment is then loaded with meaning. Not predestined in a certain way but carrying potentiality in the making.

The impersonal side, on the other hand, cannot change. And it is therefore void of free will. It does not need it. In fact, it has no need at all. It is already everything.

But as said, the personal side is eternally changing, and personal entities affect and are affected by other entities in an endless interaction of events. In the personal realm, the freedom of choice, or maybe we should say the freedom of chance, is necessary. Absolute predeterminism would cause a standstill. The energy would have had no energy, which is a strange thing to say. But nevertheless, it would be the same as nothingness.

I admit that it is hard to conceive of inanimate entities having free will. We return to that issue again before the end of this book.

Chapter 13

GOD

What if God and religion are not the same?

The infinity principle stands by itself and does not need the concept of God. But existential questioning can be traced all the way back to the Palaeolithic Era[32], where prehistoric graves reveal remainders of offerings aimed towards an afterlife. Thereby they tell us that some of our earliest responses to the Big Why were to look to the skies for solace and answers. It later developed into the world religions that we know today, but the idea of a higher power, and a continuation beyond physical death has clearly accompanied human thought for as long as we know. Hence it is fair to say that godly belief has a strong and important role in the history of existential questioning. And it deserves to be treated with respect. Godly belief is quite natural to us. The old saying 'There are no atheists in foxholes'[33] indicates that even nonbelievers turn to the sky when facing sorrow, death, and despair—or when sending praise and thanksgiving, for that matter. Another old truth is that hope is the last thing to leave us. So our question must be, what is it that we hope for?

The infinity principle is no religious belief. It is simply a logical insight that tells us that reality is both infinite and inevitable. But it can be compared to religious belief. We might actually learn something. The world's dominating belief systems stem from the Abrahamic tradition (i.e. Judaism, Christianity, and Islam). All these three hold one God as the creator of the all. Even if God did not create himself.

Religious beliefs are called beliefs since they cannot be proven, which gives the infinity principle a logical advantage over the idea of a creating God. The old fun paradox says: 'An almighty God should be able to create a riddle that he himself cannot solve. Or he cannot create such a riddle. Either way, he is not almighty.' This is of course a logical problem. The infinity principle does not have this problem since it does not create. We can also ask if an almighty God can stop being God, which of course God cannot. That argument could be used against the infinity principle too since infinity cannot stop being infinite. But the infinity principle has the logical advantage again. Infinity is inevitable in a self-explanatory and naturally undoubtable way. Infinity cannot be erased even in thought and thereby wins the battle about credibility.

But what about the personal side of reality? Could that be subject to doubt? No, and let me say it out loud and clear, it cannot. According to the infinity principle, personal existence is proven by the fact that we can question it. We already know that there is oneness, and as we question it, we know that there is twoness. We know that there is a personal realm, simply because we are here to ask about it. The infinity principle also claims that the personal realm is eternal, that it has always been and that it will always be. Neither *how* nor *why* need to be asked. Existence is a fact that we can trust.

There are similarities between the infinity principle and godly belief, but there are also differences. The infinity principle is easy to explain because it does not really *do* anything. God, on the other hand, has an agenda. Thus the explanation gets more complicated. God involves a practical idea of purpose and meaning. And of course, we must agree there are practical issues to ponder. For instance, how did humans come to be? The Abrahamic tradition says that God gathered dust from the ground, and out of that dust he formed man, and through man's nostrils God breathed life. The power-of-breath metaphor is interesting. Breathing brings life, and life is a gift. Hence, breathing is a gift. But breathing is also an obligation. We cannot refrain from breathing; we thankfully do it, but it is an obligation.

The scientific genesis story says that self-organizing life formed through a mechanical process in the ocean, starting around 4.5 billion years ago, when churning molecules turned into living cells. These living cells joined forces with other cells and started the chain-reactive progress of organic life. Some 4.4 billion years later it turned into us, the Homo sapiens. It sounds plausible, but there is a glitch. The description says that life appeared due to an automatic mechanical process. It has not been proven how it produced *life,* or consciousness. So we have the biblical description of where God created the world some six thousand years ago. And we have the scientific version, which starts in an unexplained cause. The point where inanimate matter came alive is still an intellectual mystery, whether it is approached from a religious or a scientific point of view.

The infinity principle has the same predicament and cannot give a detailed answer here. However, it sticks to its guns. Both the hen and the egg are eternal in principle. Changingness in itself has no starting point. And that goes for inanimate matter, living organisms, and what have you. We are left with both the ontological and the epistemological question about how life came to be. The scientific answer is that life emerged out of inanimate matter, but the honest answer is that we don't know.

And thus we have yet to explain how and why the ever-changing personal realm appears. How and why does inevitable oneness produce the changing multitude of the personal realm? The impersonal side is uncomplicated. Twoness is trickier, which probably is why we adapted the story of a godly creation in the first place. The gap between God's and Adam's fingers in Michelangelo's famous painting points out the unexplained interaction between God and his creation.

Still, it is hard to put the idea of God aside entirely. Even atheist scientists refer to God. Albert Einstein said, 'God does not play dice,' when he argued against the quantum field theory. Stephen Hawking has suggested that science might find God sooner or later. And consider Aristotle's *theory* and *praxis*, which have roots in Indo-European linguistic history. The word *theory* stems from the Sanskrit term *deva*, which means deity. The word *praxis* stems from *prakriti*, translating into physical nature. The two terms, God and nature, metaphysical and physical, point out the two different realms. *Theory* and *praxis* in western thought has become a description of what is real and what is not. The Vedic philosophy has travelled via ancient Greece into modern scientific language. We need theoretical investigation to understand the physical world.

In Jim Holt's book *Why Does the World Exist?* (Holt 2013)[34], Jim talks to Steven Weinberg, Nobel laureate in physics in 1979. (Weinberg is the father of the so-called *standard model*, which scientifically describes the world on the atomic scale.) In the interview Weinberg says that if we use God to explain reality, we must also explain why God is good, or loving, or jealous, or whatever attributes we would give him. If we cannot explain such specifics, we are better off with a strict physical explanation, which is Mr Weinberg's preference. But even if he rejects a divine explanation, he points to something essential here.

Believing in God automatically involves believing in a righteous future, believing in a higher power, and believing in a happy ending. Or why would we want a God in the first place? And here it gets interesting. Because even if the infinity principle does not involve an outspoken God, it does involve an inbuilt positivity, an unbuilt positivity that may be translated into lovingness, happiness, joy, or bliss. Thus, the infinity principle does not reject but rather confirm divinity, even if that divinity goes without specific explanation.

I was raised a post-war atheist in a world where God was rather absent, and where science was the main explainer of the world. Still, there was spirituality around, and I wanted to understand various ideas about religion. But I did not have to look far before I found paradoxical behaviour in religious conduct. For instance, killing in the name of God has been, and still is, part of history, and it seems irreconcilable with a message of love.

Another example is the inequality between the sexes and how it has been enhanced by various religious ideas. When I expressed these frustrations before my wise friend Mazhar, his simply replied, 'Yes, you are right, but you must keep in mind that God and religion are not the same thing.' That made sense to me. Religions are many, whilst God is one. Religions are manmade, whilst God is not. One can believe in God without being religious. I find it both reasonable and welcoming.

What brings about the idea about God in the first place? Well, God exemplifies morality. The difference between good and bad. We need God as a bringer of purpose beyond our intellectual reach. It is very hard to explain God intellectually, but if we describe God as being perfect, and in the same breath admit that we are not, we have at least illumined the enigma. God must be perfect, because God must be without lack, or it had not been God. The idea of the perfect God contrasts, and thereby sort of explains the imperfectness that through our experience taint the perfectness of the one whole. This syndrome of perfectness is found in the infinity principle too. Infinity includes everything and it cannot change, and thus it can be said to be perfect. We, on the other hand, as personal entities, are in lack; we seek to improve, we try to get somewhere, we are journeying towards a goal of sorts.

The personal entity seeks personal perfection, but the personal journey in itself requires lack to even be experienced. Remember the first chapter where Swami Satyamayananda explained God as being both personal and impersonal. Also in the Bible does God turn his face towards us and lets his grace shine upon us. That is the personal God. This is where we turn in our prayers. This side of God promises a goal to be obtained, a salvation that we cannot fully understand but which we naturally believe in.

At some point or another we all wonder about the hereafter. It is a natural thing to do. The alternative is an absolute eradication of the personal self after physical death. Very few of us believe that to be true. So the personal God gives us a message of meaning and purpose, even if we cannot intellectually grasp its nature.

Nineteenth-century Bengali saint *Ramakrishna Paramhansa* (1836–86) was both a Bhakta and Jnani. In other words, he realized the ultimate truth both in heart and mind. He studied all the big religions and concluded that they were all one and the same. One God, many religions.

And long before him, the Rig Veda said, 'God is one; the ways to reach him are many.' The idea of one God and many religions, or one truth and many explanations, is not new. And of course, neither is the problem of contradictory interpretations. But what lingers is the interpretation of God being essentially good. In *The Gospel of Ramakrishna.* (Nikhilananda, 2016)[35] it is said, 'Only through affirmation, never negation, can you know him.' By *him*, God is meant, but it could also be expressed as *the ultimate good*. This quote is logical. If we ask ourselves whether reality is loving, neutral, or evil, we find that loving prevails whilst neutral and evil subside.

How do we reach this love? By being loving ourselves. That is the simplest and most direct way. When we love God, we are one with God. We can swop the term God for life, or reality, and we can swop the term love for positivity, ending up with the same result. When we merge the personal and the impersonal, then the remaining result is positive.

The infinite positive charge has no counterpart and is therefore not threatened. It can only be reached by loving acceptance. There is an old saying: 'God can only say yes', which speaks precisely about this. And in the remarkable book *A Course in Miracles* (Course in Miracles Society 2013)[36], it is explained that *the holy spirit* never prompts anyone to do the right thing because the holy spirit can only mediate ultimate truth. If the holy spirit, being God's mediator, would prompt anyone to better him or herself, it would mean that something was wrong, and that would be an illogical, yes, even impossible action. On the ultimate level, on God's level, all is well and no corrections are needed.

When we look for God's help to solve problems on the personal side, it can only be done by letting go of our personal ambitions to change reality and accept God's unconditional love freely and willingly. *Let go and let God*, as Lester Levenson[37] put it.

Only through affirmation, never negation, can we know him (God as a symbol for reality as a whole, that is). When we condemn, or speak badly, or presume to know better even about drastic problems such as war, we cannot count on God's practical help. These problems must be solved on their own level. Our personal problems must be dealt with personally. We must know what it is that we ask for. The positive force can only be understood and reached through affirmation, through positivity. God can only say yes. And he does so when we listen. To me, that is a both logical and reassuring conclusion about godly interaction. It tells us to look for the positive answer.

Chapter 14
THE MEANING OF LIFE

*In which we ask the silliest yet most
interesting question of them all.*

An existential inquiry is obliged to ask about the meaning
of life. Or why would we want to know anything at all? We
started out by introducing the Big Why, and the meaning
of life must be its most important part. We all wonder
about it, even if we usually consider it a childish question
from which we do not expect a proper answer. Be it as it
may, let us give it try. To make it comprehensible, we will
start by sorting it into three categories: Firstly, viewed
from the impersonal side; secondly, viewed from the
personal side; and lastly, out of a godly, or maybe more
accurately, spiritual perspective.

1. So what is the meaning of life as seen from the
   impersonal side? When we consider the permanent
   unchangingness of infinity, we soon realize that
   asking for the meaning of life is the same as asking,
   why is there anything at all? And this we have

already answered. Reality has not risen out of a certain meaning, simply because it has not risen at all. Since it is infinite, it has no beginning. It has never started, it is not created, and, consequently, it has no predetermined meaning. The impersonal aspect of reality does not journey towards a goal. Infinity cannot have a goal since it is limitlessly everywhere, at every time. There is no specific point where an answer can be found. Or even more accurately, the *same* answer is given at every certain point. Thus, answering the meaning of life strictly from the impersonal point of view is a very easy task indeed. There is none. But that is an unsatisfying answer to our pondering minds. And why is that? Well, we all want to find an answer and the only answer we get here, is that there is no answer, at least not that can be pointed to. There is one good thing about this conclusion though. We can confidently trust it. Infinity is reliable in that sense. And moreover, there is another, more reassuring conclusion to be drawn here. As reality is infinite, ever present, and inevitable, it is meaning in itself. Meaning then is an intrinsic part of the unchanging whole. It comes with the package, so to speak. That is quite logical. The opposite would be that reality is meaningless. And since reality, as we already have discovered, holds an intrinsic and inerasable force, it seems wrong to call it meaningless.

2. The meaning of life seen from the personal point of view is a much juicier story. Why is that? Well, here it gets personal. Every entity is from its own

point of view the centre of the universe. Every one of us is the centre from which our own personal journey unfolds. I cannot tell you your specific personal meaning, just as you cannot tell mine. But we can discuss it in a general sense. According to our own experience we are goal-oriented beings. We seek goals, and we aim for certain outcomes. We are constantly going somewhere, it may be experienced positively or negatively, nevertheless, we are on a journey, and journeys has goals. Goals equals meaning, and in that sense our lives are full of meaning. Our only remaining task is to find out what personal meaning we desire.

Before we move on to the third aspect, let us check out what science, religion, and philosophy say about this topic. And we can start with recognizing that science says nothing about meaning whatsoever. It stubbornly sticks to the *how* side of things, showing no interest in *why* issues, let alone seek a deeper meaning. The general scientific idea is that if there were a soul, if there were a deeper meaning, we would know by now. We have examined everything through and through and found no soul and can therefore proclaim that there is no such thing.

There is an old Vedic story that addresses such interpretation. It goes like this: God and man were playing hide and seek. The game had gone on for a while, and man was doing pretty well, finding things and creating new mysteries.

But now it was God's turn to do the hiding again. And God said to himself, 'This time it will be a good one, this time I hide the meaning of life.' God knew humans well. He knew people were thorough, persistent, stubborn, and curious. He knew humans would search high and low, in the deepest depths, on the highest mountaintops, and in the most remote corners. This time it had to be the perfect hiding place. God gave it a long, good thought, and finally said to himself, 'I'll hide it right here in the open. Before their very noses. That is the one place they never look.'

And sure enough, humans looked in the farthest far, and in the deepest depths. He sure was busy. God had himself a nice and snug afternoon. And in fact, humankind is still looking, still searching, never taking the time to stop, never noticing what is hidden right before their very nose.

This is a fun tale. Might be some truth in it though. The scientific method is great, on that we can all agree, but it is not suited to detect what does not need to be detected. By that I mean that even if the truth is obvious, science will keep looking. Science is great in doing what it does, but we should not count on it to tell us the meaning of life.

What about religion then? Religion has the opposite point of view. To religion, the meaning of life is essential. But it is a matter of belief. If one believes in a creating God, then God, and the belief in itself, is the meaning. And there is no need for an intellectual explanation. The meaning is already found even if it lacks intelligibly understandable reasoning. Hence, doubt may occur.

Philosophy asks, 'What is the meaning of God?' Which is the same as asking why is there anything at all?, which we have already answered. So, all in all, none of our three main faculties has an intelligibly understandable answer to offer.

If we give science one more go we find that a hard-core physicist says that all that exists is matter. And nothing more to it. If this is true, then we can compare ourselves to planets and stars. We are born, we exist, and we die. Just like planets and stars. Just like galaxies and the entire universe. Planets and stars are existing entities even if we cannot imagine what it is like to be one. Does planets and stars have meaning? Well, they are part of the universe, and the universe have meaning. At least to us. And then planets and stars can be said to have meaning. But what if we were not here? What if the universe was without consciousness, but the planets and the stars still followed their trajectories? Would they have meaning then? Well, they would travel through space, interact with their surroundings, collide with meteors, getting sucked into black holes, die of old age, evaporate into dark energy, or dark matter, or some other transition that we cannot even imagine. They would be on a journey—and journeys, as we already have concluded, have goals. And goals equal meaning. In that sense they have meaning. And then meaning happens even without us. And if we are the only ones who are conscious, then meaning occurs even if no one knows about it. If this is true for planets and stars, then it must be true for every entity. From particles to planets. And beyond. They are on a personal journey, just like us.

Another approach would be to ponder psychology. In the bestselling book *Man's Search for Meaning* (Frankl 2008)[38], psychologist Dr Viktor E Frankl draws on his own experiences from being imprisoned in a Nazi concentration camp. He proclaims that having meaning in the sense of having personal goals is our most important psychological driving force. He says that if our sense of meaning is lost, then we are prone to give up. Even under the most horrific of circumstances, which he himself knows firsthand, a sense of meaning is the one thing that can keep us going. In fact, even in the face of death, meaning can be found. He describes meaning as a constantly achievable option. And he emphasizes that it is mastered by our own will. It is in our own hands to find meaning. To live and die in *dignity*. With a sense of purpose. But it is not a static thing. He says, 'Meaning always changes but never ceases to be.' He compares it to ask a chess master for the best possible move. It comes down to the present situation; there is no best move in a general sense.

But what is meant by living and dying in dignity? Dignity comes from personal strength and is measured by an inner knowingness of right and wrong. According to Frankl, this inner knowingness is reached through our conscience. Our conscience is our compass. And from where does conscience stem? Has it developed evolutionary out of the instinct to survive, or does it have its root beyond organic life? Is it in par with Plato's idea of the good? Or is it just a physical consequence arisen out of coincidence?

I asked my wife about it all. She said, 'It seems that things gets meaning when we give them meaning.' And I agree; she is right. That is plain and simple. But it also means that we are the doers in the making of meaning, just as Frankl points out. And then, if we are the doers in the making of meaning, we are interacting on a larger scale. We are active producers of meaning in the intricate web of cause and effect.

But, the final question must be: Is there a goal beyond the now? Does our mission stretch beyond what we encounter in our personal lives? Is there an overall meaning to life or to existence as such?

3. The third category addresses whether there is a spiritual goal, a higher goal beyond the bodily experience of being a personal entity. Every religious believer, be it amongst Judaism, Christianity, Islam, *or any other path of faith*, obviously agrees with that idea. A believer in the Abrahamic story of *one* supreme God believes in heaven and hell, and in such motto, they also believe in a metaphysical realm beyond the physical. A hardcore scientist would not agree. The scientist might see the continuation of matter-bound energy as some sort of meaning in itself. But there will be no room for any higher goal. No celestial goodness beyond the present physical situation.

An example of this third category is found in the Vedic tradition. Life on Earth is described as being trapped in Samsara, which is a cycle of rebirthing on an evolutionary ladder. One either moves forward or declines depending on one's conduct within one's current existence. Samsara is likened to a wheel that rolls indefinitely. Within this wheel, existence is inescapably tainted by suffering. And subsequently, the goal, the meaning of existence is to move beyond Samsara and become liberated.

This liberation can be achieved through the path

of yoga. Yoga is described as a method with four limbs. These are Bhakti, Raja, Karma, and Jnana yoga.

Bhakti yoga is the path of devotion. The obstacle to liberation is identified as desiring worldly pleasures. And the solution is to turn these worldly desires into desiring God.

Raja yoga is the path of meditation. Here the problem is identified as a scattered mind. And the solution is to focus the mind.

Karma yoga is the path of righteous conduct. The problem is acting for selfish reasons. The solution is acting unselfishly.

Jnana yoga is the path of understanding. The problem is identified as ignorance about the true nature of reality. And the solution is to understand reality.

The aim of all these paths are to unite the impersonal and the personal sides of reality. The term Yog or yoga means to unite, unify, or connect. It is also found in English, here as yoke, in the meaning of the pairing of two oxen, or as a description of the matrimonial stake.

Swami Vivekananda came to the United States in 1893 in order to introduce the yogic path. In his first English book, *Raja Yoga* (Swami Vivekananda 2017)[39], he says, 'Each soul is potentially divine, and the goal is to manifest this divinity. Do it by one, two, three, or all the paths combined, and become free from human bondage'. Thus Vivekananda unwaveringly proclaims that life on Earth has a higher goal and that we should strive henceforth. And when we think about it, we soon see that this is what every religious or spiritual path says, and not only Hinduism but Christianity, Islam, or any other religion.

Basically, they all tell the same story: We suffer hardship, but we reach salvation if we take the right steps. We need not get into detail about the different ideologies here, but the idea of meaning is the same. There is a goal beyond our sense perceptions and that is what we journey towards. We cannot exactly know what the goal will be like, but we trust it to be there.

So what does the infinity principle say about this? It says that reality is charged with a positive force. This positive force is constant and beyond all changing circumstances in the personal realm. When we see this intrinsic positive force as our most desired goal, then we have a logically understandable goal that is attainable. How is it attainable? Well, strive towards a positive outcome. Listen to your inner voice. Your conscience, as Viktor Frankl suggested. Hear it and follow it. If we interpret our most desired goal as being loving, then reality per definition is loving. John Lennon sang, 'Love is the answer/and you know that/for sure' (Lennon 1973)[40]. John did not represent science or religion. He represented people like us. He represented ordinary common sense.

By contemplating the infinity principle, we find the core of reality where the impersonal and the personal merges into one. We can still ask why infinity is infinite, but this particular *why* we must live with; this why we must accept; this why is intrinsic. It is answered only by the fact that it is infinite. And so, all in all, the meaning of life is to merge the positive force. That is at least how I interpret the infinity principle.

Chapter 15

BLAISE PASCAL

An existential inquirer meets a kindred spirit of thought.

We have consulted all three main faculties—science, religion, and philosophy—on our journey so far. Now we shall meet a man who embodies all three disciplines. My first encounter with this extraordinary person was through a quote from his writings: 'In deep space the universe engulfs me, reducing me to a pinpoint, but through thought I can understand that universe.' It talked directly to my own comprehension of the world. I had to know more about the man who could utter such a phrase. And I was not disappointed.

Blaise Pascal (1623–62) was a French polymath and child prodigy who, despite a short lifespan, accomplished many great things. He constructed theorems and commenced scientific experiments that are still valid today. He was an inventor and an engineer. He designed and constructed Paris's first omnibus system. At an early age he designed and constructed the world's first automatic calculation device, the Pascaline, a forerunner, one might say, of computers to come.

He was a scientist and true to the scientific method. At the same time he was a philosophical theologian who was greatly involved in the quarrels over whether God exists. It was an infectious topic that actually sent people to jail for posing the wrong opinions. He authored a series of widespread writings about it. These writings are still known today as *The Provincial Letters*. They are greatly respected, both for their reasoning and for their prose.

But he did not only debate theology. He was also one of the originators of probability calculation. And as we soon will see, these two fields in combination are of special interest to our inquiry.

Probability calculation is all about calculating probable outcomes and future results in a rational way. It has an enormous impact on our society today. It drives voting and election strategies, insurance fees, marketing campaigns and commercials, Facebook algorithms, lobbying, online betting, gambling—you name it. It is also a fundamental function in AI as it drives the self-generated strategies these machines use to respond to our desires.

Pascal was interested in odds and in betting. He invented the roulette machine even if that particular invention came as a byproduct out of a failed attempt to build a perpetual device. Now we might ask ourselves what an existential inquiry has to do with gambling? Well, in the story of Blaise Pascal the answer is everything.

And what is more, it connects directly to the infinity principle.

Let us first hear a brief background story about this man. His mother died when he was three, and he was raised by his father and two sisters. The family were Christian, and especially one of his sisters, Jacqueline, had a strong inclination towards religious life. Especially Jainism, which was an influential and provocative line of thought at the time. Blaise's father was of good rank, and Blaise himself was celebrated and respected amongst intellectuals in his capacity as a mathematician and an able engineer. Thus, Pascal was an inventor, a philosophical debater, and a personal believer, highly and successfully involved in the issues of his day.

But something happened. Around the age of thirty he was involved in a traffic accident. It seemed to have brought a deeply personal religious revelation of sorts. He referred to it as the Night of Fire, in which he seemed to have reached a personal certainty about his own godly belief. He took it very seriously. He kept notes from the event sewn into the pocket of his jacket. He started to withdraw towards a secluded lifestyle where he concentrated on exploring his experience in contemplation and in writings.

He had poor health throughout life, and he died in bed at the age of thirty-nine. He left behind a big number of notes and writings. These writings were aimed as a logical apology for Christian belief. He did not get to finish them, but seven years after his death they were collected and released as *Pensées* (Pascal 1995)[41]. Pensées translates to *thoughts*. It raised great interest at the time it was released, and it is well-known to this day. Its most famous piece is called 'The Wager'. Pascal presents a rational thought connection between the knowable and the unknowable.

And he presents it as a bet. He took his own experience and personal intuitive insight and combined it with his intellectual interest in probability calculation. And he proposed an intriguing conclusion.

The sought-out problem is whether we can know if God exists. Pascal admits that we cannot. We can neither prove nor falsify the existence of God with absolute certainty. In other words, man's knowingness cannot give us the correct answer. Hence, our only remaining option is choosing what to believe. This was true then, and it is still true today.

Pascal points out that we know that there are infinite numbers even without knowing their nature. Is it odd or even? Thus we can also claim to know that God exists without being able to show how.

We know that there is an answer, but we don't know what it is. We are caught in the same fork as so many times before. We cannot know, and at the same time we cannot let go of wondering. And it is here that Pascal, the gambler and master of probability calculation, suggests an interesting and rational thought experiment. Does God exist or not? What is the rational bet? A coin is spun. It is a 50/50 chance. Pascal sets out the rules as such: We are not allowed to stand back. We are not allowed to pass. We are obliged to play. Now, what are the odds?

It is a fourfold possibility:

1. We bet for God's existence. And God does exist. We win an infinity of bliss.
2. We bet against God's existence. But God does exist. We risk eternal misery.

3. We bet for God's existence. But God does *not* exist. Status quo, we neither win nor lose.
4. We bet against God's existence. And God does *not* exist. Again, status quo, we neither win nor lose.

Pascal concludes that betting on the positive choice, that God exists, is the most rational bet. Either we win an infinity of bliss, or alternatively, nothing happens. We do not lose anything, we are stuck in the same rut, status quo. It is therefore a safe bet. And we should stake all we have. In other words, we ought to stake our lives upon a positive belief. It should be remembered that for Pascal, believing in God and living accordingly yielded eternal happiness in heaven, whilst the opposite involved the risk of eternal damnation when one's time on Earth was up. But Pascal also adds a bonus payoff to be collected already in this life. A bonus payoff yielded by the fortunes coming from being faithful, honest, humble, and a sincere good friend. Which he sees as attributes of a godly and unselfish state of mind.

Pascal ties earthly and heavenly pursuits together through a combination of sound reasoning and scientific method. And he puts it into action by spinning a coin. I love it. It is just neat. And I am not the only one who is intrigued by Pascal's reasoning. There are a shipload of articles, writings, and debates, from long ago and up to this day. Stanford Encyclopaedia of Philosophy[42] provides a rich preview for anyone interested.

There are of course loads of objections against Pascal's reasoning. They mainly revolve around Pascal's belief in a Christian God. It is pointed out as exclusive towards other belief traditions. And what's more is that Pascal's reasoning involves a certain idea of what is meant by being good. And that is a premise that can be interpreted in different ways. I don't care so much about this discussion. To me it is more about the principle than about the details. Faith and personal preferences about how life ought to be led will always differ.

Blaise Pascal touches upon an essential existential issue, and I honour him for it. Even if his framing may seem unfortunate. Blaise Pascal faces an age-old epistemological question against religious belief. How do we know that there is a God? How do we know that our ideas are true?

Here it is interesting to see that the infinity principle does not have this problem. The phenomenon of infinity is neither a scientific truth nor a belief. It is a truth beyond doubt. According to the infinity principle, existence has no final ending and therefore it do not contain neither an eternal heaven nor an eternal hell. You might argue that heaven and hell are infinite too. But according to the infinity principle, that is impossible. At least in the personal realm. If there were an eternal heaven, what would it be like? It would have been perfect. But for how long? Forever?

The infinity principle says that such perfectness cannot be, since unchanging perfection equals absolute equilibrium, absolute equilibrium equals nothingness, and nothingness is impossible. The same goes for the eternal penance in burning flames. If someone was to burn in pain forever, it would eventually become routine, fade into boredom, and ultimately into nothingness.

Eternal penance does not work any better than eternal perfection as an explanation of existential purpose.

Understand me correctly here: reality is as it is. In its unchangingness it is already perfect. Positively so. It cannot be otherwise. But that is seeing it strictly from the impersonal point of view. A personal heaven cannot be perfect since everything personal is changing. If it was not changing, and hence had no opposites, it had not been subject to personal experience. It had been dead.

The songwriter and Nobel Laureate, Bob Dylan, touches upon this subject in his song 'Visions of Johanna' (Dylan 1966)[43]. One line goes, 'Inside the museums, infinity goes up on trial, voices echoes, this is what salvation must be like after a while.' I cannot help but picturing Dylan standing in the Louvre, looking at the eternal masterpieces, (*Mona Lisa* is mentioned in the song) thinking, *how long does an eternal masterpiece stay a masterpiece?* And back at his chamber, expanding on it, asking, *how long is salvation?*

We all wish for eternal happiness, which the concept of salvation is all about. But for how long can we be perfectly happy? Dylan recognizes this dilemma. Pascal's reasoning is not the same, but I sense kindred thought. They both looked for reason beyond the ordinary. Dylan still does.

Be as it might, I wish to propose a similar bet to Pascal's *The Wager.* Instead of waging for or against God's existence, we bet for or against intrinsic purpose. We do not need to question whether reality is positive at its core. That we already know. We ask whether there is an inbuilt purpose to existence or not. This is the root question when we ask about the meaning of life. At the end of the day, the ultimate existential question must be, 'Is there an inbuilt purpose to existence?' Followed by, 'Are we, as people, responsible for its fulfilment?'

The alternative is not nonexistence since nonexistence is impossible. The alternative is existential meaninglessness in the way a strict physicalistic worldview foretells. So, on one hand *an* achievable purpose to life, on the other hand utter meaninglessness.

We spin the coin, and we make our bets. Again, it is a fourfold setup.

1. We bet in favour of an existential purpose. And there is one. We can rest assured that our journey is worthwhile and that our purpose is positive.
2. We bet against an existential purpose. But it is there. We risk ongoing mistrust and uncertainty.
3. We bet in favour of an existential purpose. But there is none. Status quo, we neither win nor lose.
4. We bet against an existential purpose. And there is none. Again, status quo, we neither win nor lose.

The ground conditions are the same as for Pascal; we cannot know the answer; we have to take it on faith and trust our intuition. In order to see this reasoning clearly, it is important to remember the division between the impersonal and personal side of things. There is a difference between the terms reality and existence here. Reality represents the impersonal unchanging side, including everything within the infinite whole. Existence represents the personal changing side in which timebound personal entities operates. The impersonal side is not being valued here. It is what it is. It is positively charged, but not as opposed to any negation. It is positive through and through.

The personal side on the other hand is driven by ongoing change and is experienced through the fluctuation between good and bad. Whether we can grasp experience amongst inanimate entities or not doesn't change the principle of the personal side, the same ground conditions of timebound change applies. The bottom-line question is not whether reality is positive or not. As already said, that we know. Our question is whether personal entities, including ourselves, have a mission to fulfil.

Of course, we face the same uncertainty that Pascal confronted. As personal entities, we must change, and it cannot be entirely positive. But our aim, our purpose, can be aimed towards the positive side, towards the ultimate good. What are the alternatives? Anger and apathy. Unsatisfied desire.

I return to John Lennon's, 'Love is the answer', Ramakrishna's, 'Only through affirmation, never negation, can we know God', or Plato's idea of an ultimate good. There is an ultimate good. Also on the personal changing side, we know it intuitively. Then believing in a purposeful loving meaning of life, and acting accordingly, is the accurate thing to do. After having followed Blaise Pascal's example, we know that it is so, not only because it feels good, but because it is the rational and logical bet.

Chapter 16

THE SURVIVAL INSTINCT

The most mysterious mystery.

We have discussed a number of mysteries already. Free will, consciousness, and time for instance. Yet, this next topic beats them all. The survival instinct takes us to the brink of our deepest imagination and compels us to question the very motivation behind organic life.

I posed this question to my good friends at the breakfast table recently: 'Why do we have a survival instinct?'

They looked at me as if I had now finally lost it completely. One of them said, 'We need it to stay alive, dummy. Is there anything else you want to know? Or can we just enjoy our coffee, please.'

Now, that is an exciting response. One thing I have learned is that when something is taken for granted with such absolute obviosity that doubt don't even occur, then it carries some profound realness.

Despite all the hours I spent listening to scientists, philosophers, spiritual debaters, and theologians, never once did I hear the survival instinct being questioned. It is treated as such obvious fact that it defies every need of explanation. We put tremendous effort into understanding gravity, electromagnetism, nuclear energy, quarks, and bosons. And living cells and organic replication. But the survival instinct is never mentioned. It is unquestioned and undoubted. And yet it is the cause behind our most fundamental driving forces as well as our grandest attempts to civilize the entire universe. So when my friends teasingly asked, 'Is there anything else you want to know?'—well, yes, there is! I want to know the mechanics behind this force that underpins our very existence.

Before we plunge ourselves into this tantalizing enigma, I must warn you. This is not a detective story that will be solved in the end. Logically, there must be an answer, but I am afraid that we will not find it. But having said that, this is an existential inquiry, and we cannot stop ourselves from asking. Why do we want to survive? The very question may seem like blasphemy, or at least a rather nihilistic approach. Yet in order to sincerely understand existence at its most fundamental level, we must ask why we so dearly treasure it.

The survival instinct seems to be built into organic life since day one. We do not know how cells came alive in the first place, but scientists talk of LUCA (last universal common ancestor), which simply says that a descension down the path of evolution leads to one first type of cell out of which every other cell, and then all organic life, stem. LUCA is the last unit in the chain of evolution. Last, as seen looking backwards from our point of view, but first as seen from its own point of view. We do not only share a humanoid common ancestor, but the entire organic community stem out of one single cellular kind. The ingredients of these small building-blocks are fairly well understood, even how they technically may have joined together into the sort of units we call cells. But how they came alive, and how they began to duplicate and replicate into compounds of living organisms is a mystery, as we already have been talking about. And somewhere in this process the survival instinct appeared. This is what bugs me. What ignited the instinct to survive?

Here we have a resemblance to a detective story. Why, how, and when, did the survival instinct spring into action, and who is responsible? Let us briefly consider these questions.

Why? Why did the survival instinct evolve in the first place? Could life not just have been worth striving for without adding anxiety and death-fear into the equation? Could it not have been worthwhile for the sheer amazement of it?

How? The *how* question is the successful trademark of the scientific method, but at this point it leads into the blue. The old joke about the scientific method is appropriate here: 'Give us one free miracle and we explain the rest.'

When? At what point did the survival instinct step on to the scene? This is the ultimate hen and the egg question. Which came first? Either the incitement for survival instinct was already there somehow, or it developed as the cells developed. If it developed as the cells developed, it should have been out of an evolutionary advantage. Now, the driving force behind evolutionary progression is usually explained by help of the survival instinct. But if the survival instinct was not there yet, what force compelled it to rise?

Finally we get to the *who* question. There seems to be two options available: either the survival instinct came from some sort of metaphysical sphere, or it arouse out of crude physics.

If it was the latter, then it must already have been there before the first cells formed. It would mean that some sort of potentiality for life awaited dormant in the inanimate world. It almost seems to imply that stones also have survival instinct somehow, which is quite a stretch even for a vivid imagination as my own. Who is the who lurking here? As Pascal said, we cannot know; neither common sense nor science can give us the answer.

Spiritual explanations of course provide plenty of answers. And Abrahamic belief provides one specific answer. But if God created life, then it seems that he must have added the survival instinct for a reason. God himself cannot need a survival instinct, which would be ridiculous. God must be confident in his beingness, whilst we poor beings are under the spell of the survival instinct. And then we are back at the why question. Our investigation has so far led to an open end where your guess is as good as mine.

But open ended or not, the infinity principle is open ended too, in a sense. And yet it is intelligibly understandable. In my futile, still relentless attempts to find intelligible explanations about the personal side of reality, I tend to turn to science in hope for their supremacy. Sometimes it works out well, and sometimes it don't. The survival instinct in particular is one of the topics where science misses the mark. Yet it will be interesting to hear what some scientists have to say.

In his book *The Selfish Gene* (Dawkins 1976)[44], which came top on the Royal Society's poll over the most influential scientific book of all times, author Richard Dawkins extends the theories about evolution as presented by Charles Darwin in his *The Origin of Species* (Darwin 1859)[45]. According to the evolution theory, every specie, every branch of genes, tries to survive, and those who are best at it wins. But then we must ask ourselves, what do they actually win? And it seems they win the opportunity to reproduce. It tells us that organic life is nothing but a succession of genes. But does that really explain the survival instinct?

Here the survival instinct illumines the differences between an existential inquiry and a scientific explanation. An existential inquiry asks about a deeper purpose of life, which science doesn't. I respect the scientific attitude of avoiding speculation, but from a deeper existential point of view it leads to a dead-end street. Richard Dawkins ensures us that there is nothing hidden in any metaphysical realm and that the physical realm is all that there is. Everything that happens, happens due to a physical succession where the sole purpose of life is the prosperity of able genes and where living entities are nothing but machinery vehicles in the service of these genes.

But when Richard Dawkins is interviewed by Lex Fridman in Lex's brilliant podcast[46], he is asked about the meaning of life. Dawkins starts his answer by saying that the meaning of life is the propagation of genes, which of course is his already expressed standpoint, and which is the same as saying that there is no meaning at all. Life is nothing but a mechanical process. But then he continues by admitting that we all have personal goals, such as winning a football match, writing a book, cook a meal for a loved one, and so forth. These are of course ideas that we all can recognize. But, and this is interesting, he then adds that some of these goals are noble goals. And I ask myself *What can possibly be meant by being noble in a reality that has no other purpose than reproducing genes?* If it is all programmed into our brains genetically, it seems that attributes like being noble lack any proper value.

Unfortunately, he is not asked about the survival instinct, so we get no specific answer about that. But he is asked about something similar. He is asked about his feelings towards his own mortality. He admits being sad about the fact that he will have to leave. And then he goes on to say that the dark and frightening side of mortality is the idea of eternity. Eternity, he says, goes on for billions and billions of years, and he concludes by saying, 'The best way to spend it is under a general anaesthetic, which also is what it will be.' He sticks to his guns. His body is a vehicle for genes and there is nothing more to it. But why does he dread eternity?

Another scientific theory further emphasizes the mechanistic explanation. It suggests that motherly love has developed to enhance our chances to survive. Animals with babies that needed extensive care stood a better chance to survive if the mother had feelings for it. So that was the reason why love for one's children initially arose. Motherly love then is nothing but a crude mechanism of evolution and has nothing to do with love in any noble way. It simply feeds the beast, the beast being the survival instinct. This idea fits well into the strict materialistic explanation where no soul or deeper purpose is present. But it erases all value of nobleness in motherly love. In fact, it reduces all nobleness, love, beauty, kindness, compassion, and splendour into the sole purpose of reproducing the gene.

But there are also other, different scientific theories. One comes from Harvard professor Richard Wrangham, author of *The Goodness Paradox* (Wrangham 2020.)[47] Richard has done extensive research on chimpanzees and other big apes. He points to instinctive aggression as a significant and interesting evolutionary ingredient of organic life, not only for animals but also for the human species. Professor Wrangham describes aggression as being either reactive or proactive. Reactive aggression is lashing out spontaneously, whilst proactive aggression is deliberate thought-through aggression set in play to enhance power in a larger sense. He suggests that Homo sapiens have learned to control and downplay reactive aggression, whilst we at the same time have maintained and even enhanced the capability of intricate proactive aggression. He even suggest that the success of the Homo sapiens is partly due to the ability to use deliberate proactive aggression. Harassed individuals got together to kill bullies and tyrants for the sake of the common good. Beta males learned to join forces in order to kill the dictatorial Alpha male. Furthermore, this may also have been an evolutionary advantage as it opened up for improved communication.

This points to something interesting. If we have learned to control our reactive aggression, is it then possible to also change our tendency of proactive aggression? By downplaying reactive aggression, we have changed an instinctual behaviour. If we can change our instinctual lust for power and selfish fulfilment unto a path of loving kindness, it would be a significant shift in the story of our evolution.

When professor Wrangham was interviewed by Anders Hansen[48] for Swedish Television about the notions of good versus evil, Professor Wrangham suggested that even if we have the instinctual ability to kill our fellow human, we both can, and should, *move beyond our instincts*, especially when it comes to aggressiveness and hostility.

It somehow indicates another purpose behind it all. A purpose of another kind than a mere reproduction of genes. The description of the gene behaviour must not be wrong. But there might be more to the picture than meets the eye. There might be another kind of evolution that calls us along.

We have so many fears, *and the root of fear is the fear of death*. The fear of death derives from the survival instinct. As seen from a human perspective the survival instinct is responsible for a lot. It drives our longing for security as well as explains why we always want more. Our longing for increased material wealth is not firstly a longing for blissful happiness. It is driven by our fear of death. The survival instinct is responsible for the immoderate greed that brings about horrendous injustice in this world and the overuse of resources that may lead us to the brink of disaster. If we would understand and master this instinct, then we would be on to something fantastic. That would be a shift in paradigm worth mentioning. Is it doable? I don't know. But it is worth considering.

Humans can do a lot, no doubt about that. *But we did not create reality.* We did not create existence. We did not create life. The scientific dogma says that life emerged mechanically out of a prehistoric soup. But life arrived late in this universe. We act as if we are its main purpose. But are we? Life on earth is a flickering moment in the infinite perspective. Trying to grasp an origin calls for humbleness. We participate in a swirling dance set in motion by a force much stronger than a personal entity can grasp completely. That is a cause for humility.

But we are also powerful beings on a mission. To understand our role in reality we must understand our mission. The survival instinct holds a major role in that scheme.

Do planets and stars have a 'star heaven' where they go when they die? Do they dread eternity, hoping for a general anaesthesia, like Richard Dawkins does? This question is beyond intelligible imagination. Nevertheless, planets are real. And they were here long before we were. Why does organic life have survival instincts when inanimate matter does fine without it? It lacks an intelligible answer. Still, we must ask it. Do inanimate entities care if they exist or not? We don't know. Can it be that within this enormous universe, with all its splendour and multiplicity, we are the only ones who care?

The survival instinct urges us to ask about a higher purpose. But not even spiritual traditions explain the survival instinct. If life is a test towards an afterlife of sorts, if we are here to learn something, if we have a mission with a purpose, is the role of the survival instinct to make sure that we endure the test? If we were not compelled to do it, would we simply refuse? Organic life endures tremendous hardships to stay alive and to reproduce. There are pleasures involved, but the fear of death is stronger than the desires for pleasure. How and why did it emerge? The survival instinct compels us to contemplate the driving force behind evolution.

What caused sapiens to ask the Big Why in the first place? Is there a yet hidden evolutionary reason? Is it beneficial to our genes' reproduction? Or is it merely an unfortunate evolutionary detour, soon to be obsolete?

Or may it be that it holds another purpose? Does the why question have evolutionary significance beyond our intellectual understanding? If there is a deeper goal beyond physical survival, the why question may be an evolutionary step in that direction, an evolutionary advantage on a whole other scale. The survival instinct sure is an intriguing topic.

What does the infinity principle have to say about it? Just like Richard Dawkins, the infinity principle sticks to its gun. It says that the impersonal side of reality cannot change. So, as seen from that perspective the survival instinct is a non-issue. The unchanging side of reality do not need survival instinct. It has nothing to lose, nothing to fear. It cannot be threatened.

But the personal side is another story. The personal side is affected by this mystery. Here we long, fear, and hope for something better. We call it existence.

The infinity principle gives no specific answer about the purpose of the survival instinct. But the fact that we are able to ponder this issue at all seems to suggest a purpose in itself. It indicates an extension beyond the scientific dead-end street.

If there is a higher purpose to existence, as was suggested in the chapter about the meaning of life where transcendence from physical bondage was mentioned, a transcendence that can be called *enlightenment*, *Nirvana*, or *going to heaven*. If such an idea is real, which it might be, then we face a delicate assignment: Namely, to proceed beyond the physical reality of existential bondage. The infinity principle has an open door here. Even if no detailed description is given.

The survival instinct surely is a mystery. And I foretell that we will find reason to contemplate it further still.

Anyhow, to wrap it up, this was meant as a serious discussion, still I wish to finish it on a somewhat lighter foot by serving you yet another Vedic story. It goes like this:

Once upon a time, long before humans walked the earth, it so happened that God was alone. Nothing disturbed him and everything was perfect. If maybe a bit boring. God felt the need to amuse himself. And he decided to play hide and seek. But as he was alone, who was he to play with?

God is of course very clever, and he found a solution. He said, 'I pretend that I am not God, and then I go looking for God.' Said and done. He thrust himself into action. Now, this was good fun. God soon got so immersed in the game that he forgot that he knew the answer. And the search goes on …

Chapter 17

ACCEPTANCE

In which we locate the exit to the other realm.

In this chapter we will draw a picture in our minds to help us understand the connection between the changing and the unchanging sides of reality. This task is abstract, and our personal interpretations may very well differ. Still, I hope we find something to share. And it is important that we try. Without some sort of understanding, without a picture in our minds, we keep carrying this riddle as an unsolved enigma, keeping us in existential doubt, maybe even existential anxiety.

Recently a rather strange sentence appeared in my mind. It read: *Existence ends at acceptance.* In the moment I understood it, but when I wrote it down it sounded odd. Let me try to explain. We started this chapter by saying that we should try to find the borderline between the personal and impersonal realms. The place where the realm of changingness meets the realm of unchangingness.

We should remember that the infinity principle says that *existence* belongs to the personal/changing side.

Whilst *infinity* and *eternity* constitute the unchanging/impersonal side, we should also remember that existence means *to be standing out*, to be changing. Infinity and eternity do not stand out. They are the unchanging backdrop.

Existence, including every kind of evolution, constantly changes. Some of it goes fast and some of it goes slow, but it always changes. When an existing entity—you or me, for instance—directly confronts the unchangingness of reality, something unusual happens. Again, we must be clear about that the infinite and eternal sides of reality are unchangeable. That is a fact that the personal entity cannot alter. Hence, there is nothing that the personal entity can do either to it or with it. And thus the personal entity is left with only one option, which is to accept it.

It may not sound that dramatic, but it is. It goes against our instincts. The personal changing entity has arrived at the borderline. At the end station. To cross the border, to get off the train, to fully enjoy the freedom, we have but one choice. We must accept the terms and leave all personal belongings behind. In that sense *existence ends at acceptance*.

To make this thought practically usable we must recognize the difference between infinite acceptance and everyday acceptance. Everyday acceptance is something that we do. It requires some sort of effort on our behalf. Furthermore, it is usually seen as a sign of weakness. It is surrendering to an enemy that we cannot conquer. And this we don't like. We want it our way. And of course, in everyday life we are supposed to take action and to stand our ground. It is often the right thing to do, not always maybe, but often. There are things that we should not accept. Within ourselves. Or within others. At the *personal side* we are fully responsible for our actions as well as our reactions. We must conduct this responsibility as best as we can.

So, on the personal side, accepting is something that we *do.* But on the impersonal side, acceptance is quite different. There is nothing to be done. Here acceptance is not a deed. It could rather be likened to a state of beingness. Ultimate acceptance is the mergence into oneness.

As personal entities or separated beings, we experience incompleteness. Some sort of lack. There is a weakness. And it makes us vulnerable. When we realize that we are part of the one whole, we master that weakness. We master the sense of lack. And we willingly, unselfishly, start to serve the one whole.

The task is to master the weakness, the incompleteness, and finally let go. Surrendering ourselves into the bosom of the one. Accepting even that we cannot accept everything. It may seem like a contradiction of terms. But it also reveals the depth of the exercise.

I try to do it proudly and willingly. Not as a beggar. I keep my heart and mind open. Such is my personal invocation. I don't know if it is of help to anyone else.

But let me share a concrete example from my own life. It may seem far-fetched, but it was very real to me. I had a period in my life when I was sad and anxious and felt mistreated. I accused the world and found reasons to do so. I found flaws in my parents, flaws in my teachers, flaws in society, and flaws in myself. I thought about my relationship with my father, remembering occasions when he was unbalanced and treated me poorly. At first I found him guilty of ruining my life. But then I realized that I had also been there. That I had allowed myself to be affected in such a way. And I committed myself to go back in memory as far as I could to reclaim the responsibility for my own reactions. It went well at first, but then I ran into trouble. I lost track since as a small child there are moments that one could not control. I could not even remember them. So how could I take responsibility for these moments? I felt stuck. I was affected by circumstances that I could do nothing about. It seemed to be a lost cause.

But I kept going. And I allowed atonement and forgiveness both to myself and to my father. Beyond what I could remember. Beyond what I could possibly know. And it led to acceptance. In the far end, no one was to blame. And the whole situation dissolved into bliss. And into a healing process of lovingkindness.

This was a personal story of, let us say, psychological nature. Let us now try another point of view and take an example from the Vedic tradition and a notion called *neti-neti*. Neti-neti literally means *not this and not this*. It sounds rather tiny at a first hearing, but if we take on the effort to test it as a thought-experiment, we see that it is a comprised package of wisdom. It illumines the fact that when we look for the ultimate truth, when we seek the ultimate solution to the fault of the world, when we turn every stone to see what is hidden beneath, we find that there is always yet another stone. This is neti-neti. Not this, and not this.

In other words, no matter how cleverly we point

towards the ultimate truth, it will still not be it. This is because the pointing in itself requires a pointer. A pointer at one end, and a target at the other. A seeker at one end, and something sought for at the other. That is the recipe for twoness. We do not reach oneness because we are occupied by the act of reaching. The effort makes us stuck in the effort. We feel that there is something we must do, that we are responsible for the well-fare of reality. But we are not. We cannot affect the infinite side of reality. At this point our mission is over. Here we got one option, and one option only. To accept it as it is. The entrance lies in the gap between this-and-this.

It is tricky. Letting go of resistance is not an easy thing to do. We must set aside our ego. Let us check out another example from the eastern thought-tradition. The awakened Buddha proposed a notion that he called the Golden Middle Way. It tells us that the greatest benefits are not to be found in the extremes, as in being best, or in being worst. The Golden Middle Way leads inwards to the centre, to the heart of beingness. That is where it all comes together, that is where it all merges into one. If we play around a bit with the Golden Middle Way, we end up with, 'Being good is better than being best', which sounds crazy, but which actually carries a-whole-lotta truth. Good is centred, whilst best is an extreme. Or as Jimmy Cliff[49] had it, 'The harder they come, the harder they fall'.

The idea of the Golden Middle Way also provokes us to consider our current lifestyle of untamed consumerism. But that would be discussing details and not properly suited in an existential inquiry about principles.

Yet it is funny. We willingly accept the multilayered

and complex diversity of the personal realm and at the same time find oneness incomprehensible. Should it not be the other way around? Should not oneness be easy to understand, and complex diversity seem strange. But that is probably just me and my faiblesse for abstract notions. Of course, we feel at home amongst diversity as it is the domain in which we stand.

And at the end of the day, the two sides are one. We feel that we are here, whilst the one is over there. That is just our personal limitation. We are the one pointing to itself. It is completely incomprehensible, yet absolutely logical.

We are blessed with the option to accept it. And then we fall effortlessly into bliss. Swami Vivekananda described night-motts flying straight into the flames of his nightly fire, giving themselves up in the attraction of the immense light of the consuming flames. We do not need to be that brutal to ourselves, but eventually we cannot do anything but surrender.

So this chapter ends where it started. Namely, *existence ends at acceptance.* Existence does not end in itself. Existence is eternal. It cannot cease to be. But it will be good to know that it takes place on a backdrop of infinite bliss. We are absolutely safe. On the personal side we still have our problems, but beyond that we are safe. We are always welcome home.

Chapter 18

UNCONDITIONAL LOVE

In which the light finally comes shining through.

In the last chapter, we threw our egos into the consuming fires of redemption. We reached the point where nothing could be said or done. Reality must be accepted as is. But that is not an entirely appealing future prospect. We ask, what is in it for us? What awaits us in the far end of the journey? And what is that perpetual positive charge that the infinity principle keeps bragging about?

I call it bliss. Bliss is a wonderful notion. Even though it may seem a bit abstract and vague. It does have a positive ring to it. We don't dread bliss. But can we really understand it?

We can swap it for something that is closer to us. Love. Love is our most desired goal. Everybody wants love. To get it. To give it. And to have it. But love comes with a price. We need to do something to get it. When we give it, we want something in return. There is also selfless love. Motherly love. But motherly love too comes with a price.

Sadness, worry, longing. This kind of love is not perpetual. It is not an indestructible charge. It has negative sides.

If reality is perpetually positively loaded it should reflect somehow. Perpetual means unchanging. Infinite unchangingness must be effortless. This is true for bliss. Bliss does not involve an effort. It gives freely, without an agenda.

Thus, we cannot equal bliss with *ordinary* love. We must go deeper. There is yet another layer. And I think you know what I am aiming for. It is in the title of this chapter. Unconditional love. The term *unconditional* describes the term bliss very well. I don't care if religious dogma claims that bliss must be deserved. Bliss in itself is effortless. The term unconditional translates into appearing without a price. No strings attached. Absolutely free. Unconditional love is blissful, joyous, limitlessly abundant. And always present. Even when we don't notice it.

Unconditional love is never threatened. It has no enemies. It does not push itself onto anything. It only gives. Effortlessly. Everyday love, wonderful as it is, may still be feeble and shifting. Unconditional love is not.

Paradoxically enough, for precisely these mentioned reasons, unconditional love goes by unnoticed. It involves no threat. We cannot lose it. Therefore we miss it. This sounds counterproductive. And it is.

We desire love but fear missing it instead of embracing it and being it. It can be explained by the fact that personal experience is dependent on opposites. If there were no darkness, the light had not been noticed. Bliss and unconditional love had been there, alright. But no one had known. At least not in a personal way. That is why the infinity principle is twofold. So that we can understand it.

And it is good to know. Even if unconditional love may seem obscured at times, it cannot go away. As reality's perpetual backdrop it can be trusted at all times. It is as unescapable as infinity itself. This is not wishful thinking. This is the factual state of affairs.

Note that there is no such thing as *unconditional hatred*. Hate does not occur without a reason. But there is such thing as unconditional love. It is an intrinsic part of beingness. Unconditional love doesn't require a reason. It is always there. Walking hand in hand with unconditional joy. To be alive in this beautiful world is simply joyous. It does not need to be explained. A kid wakes up in the morning and knows that it is going to be a great day. That joy, that unconditional love, is always there. And for the last time, we cannot ask science about this. Science has no interest in these matters. But we don't need science here. We know this within ourselves. We just need to listen. The whole is One. And we are servants in its glory.

Chapter 19
CONCLUSION

A brief summary of what has been said.

It may have been a crazy idea to begin with to try to capture the essence of reality. But infinity knocked on my door and I could not escape. So what is its essential message? Well, it says that reality is endless and that it therefore is *one*. But then it goes on to say that reality has two fundamental principles. These two principles/concepts/aspects, or whatever we choose to call them, seem contradictory. Yet they work together. Together they constitute the whole of reality. They are described as infinite unchangingness on one hand and eternal changingness on the other and are within this context titled the *impersonal* versus the *personal* side.

And furthermore, it is emphasized that this setup, this description of the basic nature of reality, can be intelligibly understood and grasped by the human intellect.

It is also said here that neither science nor religion are needed to understand this basic truth about reality. And this is important. It directly tells us two things. It tells us that reality is not a mystery, not at its basic level. And it tells us that we must not turn to any outer authority to understand what we inherently know.

What also needs to be said here is that it is not that one side is good, and the other side is bad. The fundamental principles of reality are unchangeable. Both sides play their part but the overall conclusion tells us that reality per se is good. The unescapable *isness,* the *beingness,* of reality cannot be anything but good. At the unchangeable level, it is a *positive* set-up.

Of course, this is not how we as personal entities *experience* it. We experience reality as sometimes good and sometimes bad. But that is all part of the personal side and the mechanics that underpin this *personal* experience of changingness has been described within the text.

However, we will certainly find reason to continue addressing the personal journey. That should be expected. And it should not be shunned, on the contrary, it should be embraced.

Yet, the prime message given by the infinity principle, is the understanding of the fundamental and unchanging aspect of reality. That is the safe haven to which we can always return when confronted with doubt, fear, and anxiety, on an existential level.

It should be clear that I did not invent the infinity principle. It is there for everyone to see. Reality can of course be interpreted in different ways. Physicist John Wheeler suggested the *it-from-bit theory.* It describes the universe as a file of information. Reality as a gigantic computation. There might be some truth to that. But one thing is certain; infinity in itself is not a computation. It has no on and off switch. It has no zero. It is one and one only. The rest of reality may oscillate to and fro. But the infinite side of it stays put. It has only one characteristic, and that is its positive charge.

To further contemplate the relationship between the personal and the impersonal sides, let us return to that reality has two sides. Infinite unchanging wholeness on one side, and eternally changing existence on the other. Oneness is certain. But so is twoness. As persons we have an experience of journeying. But from the infinite point of view, we cannot really go anywhere. We are both the wave on the ocean and the ocean in the wave.

Is there a purpose? We started out by introducing the Big Why. That includes a personal purpose of existence. Is there a purpose of changingness, is there a purpose of time? Different attempts have been made to describe infinite time. The Vedic tradition describes the Yugas, which are eons of time dominated by certain influences. These cycles ends and new ones starts. The Buddhists have Nirvana, which is beyond time and space. The Hopis prophecy a new phase in time. The Abrahamic linage suggests a judgment day and beyond that, eternal contentment for those who are chosen. The infinity principle has a simpler explanation. Reality has always been, and it will always be. Unchanging at its core and changing at its surface.

So does it have a purpose? Yes, I say that it does. Since reality is infinite and all-encompassing, it represents purpose in itself. It is positively charged. Thus being positive is its purpose. When we equal positivity with love then it gets closer to the human experience.

Why is there evil and fear? This is explained by the fact that personal experience requires opposites to arise. Evil and fear are mirroring factors of love. They make love visible and thereby make the personal journey come alive. It is important to note here that love prevails while evil and fear subsides.

Can we understand reality fully? I say that we can. But there will be different ways to do it. Saint Anselm of Canterbury, who was quoted in the introduction, said, '*Credo ut Intelligam*. I believe, in order to understand'. It could also be said the other way around. '*Intelligam ut Credo*. I understand, in order to believe'. The latter being my own experience.

Albert Einstein, one of the most brilliant thinkers known to mankind, repeatedly questioned our willingness to go to war against one another. He said that there must come a time when we can find a better path. I believe that is possible. And I believe that is what we must do. A loving heart is our purpose and our path. If for nothing else but for the fact that love is the strongest force.

In the name of positivity and lovingkindness, I return to the words of Ramakrishna Paramhansa once again: 'Not through negation, only through affirmation, can ultimate goodness be reached.' That is where we must put our effort. That is where we must put our intention. That is the goal towards which we must strive. Thank you, kindly.

Epilogue

We have reached the year 2024, and I still walk the streets, still pondering life's purpose. The eternal questions that I set out to unravel as a young man have proven to be just that, eternal. As a matter of fact, as it turned out, eternal questions were not questions at all; they were answers. I had found what I was looking for. It did not stop existence from revolving and rearranging itself in its ever-ongoing motion. There is no final ending. That is all right with me. The infinity principle assures me that reality at its core is positively charged. Who am I to file complaints against such a beautiful vision?

Acknowledgments

How do we know what we know? Well, we Google it, or have our AI tell us. We live in times when information is available in an unprecedented way. In a couple of hours we can get a decent picture of what has been gathered by thousands of people through thousands of years. Yet— and this must be emphasized—we must still draw the conclusions that lead us forward by ourselves.

In the completion of this book I studied a great number of scholars, thinkers, traditions, and ideas. Some are mentioned within the text, but many are not. Albert Einstein and Max Planck are central figures, followed by a long row of great scientists and researchers. Darwin and Dawkins have contributed to the understanding of organic life.

Another personal favourite that I have not mentioned much is Sir Roger Penrose (Nobel laureate in physics 2020). To me he rings through as persistent, gentle, and intelligent, a highly admirable person. He also carries a natural and humble portion of wisdom. He is of course well-known to everyone who has an interest in physics and science. He has a new idea out now that I look forward to hearing more about. It involves mathematical equations where in the large scheme of things, big equals small[50]. If such equation is proven right, it will fit nicely into the infinity principle. I also admire Penrose for his fearless conclusions based on mathematical insight leading to the unknowable. I heard him elaborate on Dobel's theorem saying that there are issues that can be mathematically proven to be unprovable. At the same time Penrose suggested that such issues can be understood.

He went on to say that he could not define what *understanding* in that sense even meant. Still he admitted relying on that same understanding to be useable and trustworthy. Such reasoning appeals to me since the term *understanding* holds special significance to the infinity principle. Penrose seems to imply that the phenomenon of understanding exceeds mathematical knowledge. I like that. It is quite logical. Especially in the light of infinity. (I must admit that I myself was never any good with maths. It seems that all my calculations, be it addition, subtraction, multiplication or division, ends up in *One*).

Furthermore, I have used numerous examples taken from the Vedic tradition. I have mentioned a number of monks from the Ramakrishna order, Swami Vivekananda, Swami Sarvapriyananda, Swami Satyamayananda. *Swami Vivekananda* is a giant and a beacon when it comes to addressing higher purpose. For more information about the wisdom that he reveals or to get an enhanced understanding of the Vedantic tradition as such, I dearly recommend the lectures by Swami Sarvapriyananda that are generously displayed on YouTube (search Swami Sarvapriyananda lectures). They are nothing short of brilliant.

And let me mention yet another monk from the same linage: Swami Ranganathananda. He has neatly summarized spiritual life into two questions. *With eyes closed, looking inwards, ask—who am I? With eyes open, looking outwards, ask, how can I help you?* That is great advice on our human journey towards fulfilment.

Poem on a Blank White Paper

In silent contemplation I tried to draw
a picture of infinity in my mind.
But how was I to do that?
I started out on a blank white paper … but then what?
Should I draw a circle, or a sphere?
Should I add arrows, or some other symbols?
I realized that infinity in itself has no centre.
No part is more significant than the other.
It is already complete in its oneness.
And I left the paper untouched. Just as I
tried to leave my mind untouched …
and it became a poem of infinity on
a blank white sheet of paper.

Notes and bibliographical data

Introductory quotes

1   Armatrading, Joan. *Visionary Mountain*. Song from the
    Album *Whatever's for Us*. Cube Records, London,1972. Lyric
    written by Pam Nestor. The song is also memorably recorded
    by Manfred Mann's Earth Band on the album *Nightingales
    and Bombers,* The Workhouse, London, 1975.
2   Swami Vivekananda. *Song of the Sannyasin* is a poem written
    and published in New York 1895. I have taken it from Swami
    Vivekananda's book *Raja Yoga. Conquering the Internal
    Nature.* Kolkata, Advaita Ashrama Publication House,
    Kolkata, 2017. The book *Raja Yoga*, (highly recommended)
    was originally published 1896 in New York and has been
    printed in several new editions.
3   Kilpi, Eeva. *Let me know if I disturb*. (Swedish: *Säg till om jag
    stör*.) Den Svenska Högtidsboken, Sweden, Stockholm, 1980.
    The poem originally comes from a book of poems titled *Songs
    of Love*, (Swedish: *Sånger om Kärlek*.) The poem, as well as
    the poet, is well-known in Scandinavia. Eeva Kilpi writes in
    Finnish. I could not find an official English translation and
    so I turned *Kerstin Holm-Lindquist's* Swedish translation into
    English freely.

Chapter 1

4   Swami Satyamayananda is one of the revered monks of the *Vedanta Society* in the US. Vedanta Society is a branch of the Ramakrishna Order of India, established in the US by Swami Vivekananda. I first attended a lecture by Swami Satyamayananda in California, Santa Barbara, and then later at the Vedanta Society in New York where I got to meet him for a personal conversation. This was in 2019.

Chapter 2

5   Hawking, Stephen/Mlodinow, Leonard. *The Grand Design.* New York, NY: Bantam, 2011.

6   Why is there something rather than nothing? Why is there anything at all? This question has haunted mankind for as long as we know. Wikipedia (https://en.wikipedia.org/wiki/Why_is_there_anything_at_all%3F) addresses the issue, giving examples of prominent scholars who has engaged in this question. Gottfried Willhelm Leibnitz, Ludwig Wittgenstein and Martin Heidegger are mentioned, and also Parmenides as being one of the very early investigators into this issue. But there are also many other examples. In my opinion the riddle is clearly answered by the Infinity Principle. Since reality is infinite, the *why-question* subsides into oblivion. Having said that, the inquiry can still be used to ponder a 'higher' purpose of existence.

7   Holt, Jim. *Why Does the World Exist?: An Existential Detective Story.* New York, NY: W. W. Norton & Company, 2013.

8   Kuhn, Robert Lawrence, born 1944. In his *Closer to Truth* series, which are generously broadcasted on YouTube, Robert Kuhn asks prominent scholars from a variety of fields about our most intriguing riddles, such as *free will, time,* and *the nature of God.* The series are co-created and co-produced by Peter Gentzels. Its first shows appeared on public television in the US in 2000. More info is reached on closertotruth.com. The question *Why is there something rather than nothing,*

can for instance be viewed in episode 306. https://youtu.be/cfmewf2DoKU?si=8bMtj6q9HTVlQUbE. Robert Kuhn has also written books on the subject.

9   Hawking, Stephen/Mlodinow, Leonard. *The Grand Design.* New York, NY: Bantam, 2011.

10 Chalmers, David, born in 1966, is an Australian professor in Philosophy and Neural Science. He works at the New York University. He is keenly involved in the research of the nature of consciousness. Information about his work is found on his website https://consc.net/

11 Susskind, Leonard, born in New York 1940, is a brilliant scientist and lecturer and I can only recommend enjoying his lectures displayed on YouTube.

Chapter 3

12 Adams, Douglas. *The Hitchhikers Guide to the Galaxy.* London: Gollancz, 2012.

Chapter 4

13 Brahman is a Vedic term used in Hinduism and describes the ultimate reality. It can be likened to a supreme God, but it must not necessarily be. Rather it represents the unlimited whole in which everything unfolds. According to Swami Sarvapriyanada, minister of the Vedanta Society of New York, the Sanskrit term *Brahman* literally translates into *the Vast.* It does not directly translate into *infinite,* even if its infiniteness is ascertained.

14 Sri Sri Ravi Shankar. *Shiva Sutras. A Commentary by Sri Sri Ravi Shankar.* Bangalore, Sri Sri Publication Trust, 2010. ISBN: 978-938059232-9 www.artoflivingshop.com. Sri Sri Ravi Shankar is the founder and the head of the Art of Living organization which is one of the world's largest NGOs (Non-Governmental Organization). Art of Living does tremendous work in a long line of countries, promoting a yogic and

compassionate lifestyle, and providing help to communities in severe need.

15 Parmenides of Elea. Pre-Socratic Greek philosopher from the early fifth century BC.

16 Rumi, Jalal Al-Din, (1207–1273) A Sufi mystic and a poet who wrote in Persian.

Chapter 5

17 Danielsson, Ulf. *Mörkret Vid Tidens Ände. (The Darkness at the End of Time)* Fri Tanke, Stockholm 2020.

18 I have already mentioned Parmenides. What more can be said is that he is the subject of Plato's dialogue named *Parmenides,* which the free internet version of the *Stanford Encyclopedia of Philosophy* (https://plato.stanford.edu/) calls the most enigmatic of all Plato's dialogues. As a comprehensive yet accessible source of information about Parmenides and most of the other classical Greek philosophers, let me recommend *Classical Philosophy* by Peter Adamson. It is the first book in a series named 'A history of philosophy without a gap", Oxford University Press 2014, Oxford, UK. Peter Adamson also creates and hosts the Podcast 'History of Philosophy without any gaps' that currently runs and until today spans more than 450 episodes. It is found where podcasts are found. Dive right in, boys and girls!

19 Holt, Jim. *Why Does the World Exist?: An Existential Detective Story.* New York, NY: W. W. Norton & Company, 2013. This book is noted as both a *New York Times* and a *LA Times* bestseller.

20 $E=mc^2$, the most well-known of all equations was brought forward by Albert Einstein in 1905. According to Bill Bryson, in his excellent book 'A Short Story of Nearly Everything' (Doubleday, UK, Broadway Books, US, 2003), very simply put $E=mc^2$ tells us that *mass* and *energy* are equal to one another. Energy is mass turned loose, and mass is energy waiting to be turned loose. C^2 equals to the speed of light multiplied by

itself which amounts to an enormous number and which among other things tells us that our bodies roughly stores as much energy as does 30 very large atomic bombs. Luckily(?) we cannot release that energy.

Chapter 6

21 Samkhya, or Sankyha, is a term that goes way back in the Vedic wisdom tradition. The second chapter of the *Bhagavad Gita* is called the chapter of *Samkhya Yoga*. The concept of *Samkhya* prompts us to analyze our *inner personal self* in order to gain knowledge and understanding about its true nature, thereby enabling us to discern between the personal and the impersonal sides of reality. The term *Yoga* in its turn, means to unite. Thus Samkhya Yoga prompts us to understand and discern between the two different sides of reality in order to reclaim the union of the two.

22 Rajagopalachari, Chakravarti. *Ramayana,* (Bharatiya Vidya Bhavan, India, Mumbai, 2015). This translation by C. Rajagopalachari was first released 1951. The 2015 print is the 55th edition. Chakravarti Rajagopalachari 1878–1972 was a prominent member of the Indian Society, a statesman, politician, writer, and a proponent for world peace and disarmament. *Ramayana* is an Indian epos originating from approximately 200 BC, even if the legend in itself is believed to be much older than so. Rama is sometimes seen as an incarnation of Vishnu, who in turn is one of the most important God's in Hinduism religious thought-tradition. But it is also said that *Rama* is not the God himself, but rather a prince endowed with divine qualities.

23 Adams, Douglas. *The Hitchhikers Guide to the Galaxy.* London: Gollancz, 2012.

24 *To be or not to be.* 'The most famous line from the world's most famous play'. The play in question is titled *Hamlet*, and it is written by William Shakespeare 1600 CE.

Chapter 8

25   Cohen, Leonard. *Ain't no Cure for Love*. From the album *I'm your Man* Columbia Records, New York, 1988.

Chapter 9

26   Swami Sarvapriyananda, Minister of the *Vedanta Society of New York*. Swami Sarvapriyanada gives an extencive number of brilliant lectures on Vedanta, displayed on YouTube. I can only recommend anyone who is interested in learning more about the Vedic thought-tradition to botanize amongst these lectures running currently from around 2019 and onwards. For a list of talks and to learn more about its profound wisdom, preferably visit website, Vedanta Society of New York. https://www.vedantany.org/

27   Adams, Douglas. *The Hitchhikers Guide to the Galaxy*. London: Gollancz, 2012.

28   Young, Niel. *Nothing is Perfect*. Song from the album *A Treasure*, Recorded at St Paul state fair, Minnesota, 1985. Released by Reprise Records, Warner Brothers, Burbank, California, USA, 2011. The song also appeared on the Live Aid concert at John F Kennedy Stadium 1985.

Chapter 10

29   Eddington, Arthur Stanley, 1882-1944, was a highly acclaimed physicist who did not shy to expand into philosophical and existential territory. He wrote a number of books. I have read an e-version of '*The Nature of the Physical World*' published by *Rare Treasures*, Victoria BC Canada, 2023. The book was originally published 1928. Here Eddington elaborates on both the new findings in physics and what philosophical implications it brings about, clearly articulating the difference between the two. Arthur Eddington's writings belongs to the public domain in the US and has by scholars been considered to be of significant interest to a broad audience.

Chapter 11

30 Mancuso, Stefano. *The Revolutionary Genius of Plants: A New Understanding of Plant Intelligence and Behavior.* Atria Books, New York, 2017. Stefano Mancuso has written several books and given talks that are available on YouTube.

Chapter 12

31 Einstein, Albert. 1879-1955 *The World As I See It.* Azeem Ahmad Khan, General Press, New Delhi, 2018. Page 14. The book *'Mien Weltbild'* by Albert Einstein was first published in 1934 with an extended edition in 1954.

Chapter 13

32 The Paleolithic Era, (early stone age) spans from 30 000- 10 000 BCE. There are no written remains from this period and conclusions are drawn from physical excavations.

33 'There are no Atheists in Foxholes'. This aphorism stem from warfare and points out that when in severe stress even 'non-believers' tend to turn to 'God'. The simile of a foxhole might seem a bit mismatched though, since foxes are known to have an escape exit in their dwellings.

34 Holt, Jim. *Why Does the World Exist?: An Existential Detective Story.* New York, NY: W. W. Norton & Company, 2013. This book was noted as both a *New York Times* and a *LA Times* bestseller.

35 Swami Nikhilananda, *The Gospel of Sri Ramakrishna, Abridged Edition.* Printed in the United States of America, Ramakrishna-Vivekananda Center, 2016. Eight printing. The book is copyrighted by Swami Nikhilananda 1942, 1948, and 1958. Library of Congress Catalog Card No. 58-8948.

36 Course in Miracles Society. *A Course in Miracles.* Published by CIMS, Course in Miracles Society, Omaha, Nebraska, 68114 USA. Original Edition Text, Pocket Edition, Copyright 2012, Third Printing 2013.

37 Lester Levenson 1909-1994 was a successful entrepreneur who became physically exhausted in his attempts to be successful. In 1952 he ended up in a severe health-condition, almost at the brink of dying. In that state he started to question his own self which led to a liberated self-realization of sorts. This realization stayed with him throughout his life and many people turned to him to hear more about his findings. Eventually it led to what today is called the *Sedona Method™*, currently explored and mastered by *Hale Dwoskin*. For further information please visit www.sedona.com

Chapter 14

38 Frankl, Viktor E. *Man's Search for Meaning.* Published in Great Britain by Rider, imprint of Edbury Publishing, London, 2008. Originally published in German 1946. Copyright Viktor E Frankl.

39 Swami Vivekananda. *Raja Yoga. Conquering the Internal Nature.* Advaita Ashrama Publication House, Kolkata, 2017. (This book was originally published 1896 in New York and have seen several new editions.) Swami Vivekananda has written several books on the topic of Yoga and the Veda's, paramount in explaining and promoting the Vedic thought-tradition. He came to the US in 1893 where he participated in the World Parliament of Religion in Chicago with great success. His extensive work is valid and richly acclaimed to this day.

40 Lennon, John. The song *Mind Games.* From the Album *Mind Games,* Record Plant Studios, New York, 1973. John Lennon sang about love throughout his career. In the early records it was mostly about love between a boy and a girl, but it developed into the concept of love as a universal idea. He repeatedly returned to the message; *Love is the Answer.*

Chapter 15

41 Pascal, Blaise. *Pensées.* Penguin Group, London, 1995. This translation from French was first made in 1966. Revised edition 1995.

42 https://plato.stanford.edu/entries/pascal-wager/ The Stanford Encyclopedia of Philosophy is a rich and vast source of information freely displayed on the internet.

43 Dylan, Bob. *Visions of Johanna.* Song from the album *Blonde on Blonde,* Columbia Records, Nashville Tennessee, 1966.

Chapter 16

44 Dawkins, Richard. *The Selfish Gene.* Oxford University Press, 1976.

45 Darwin, Charles. *The Origin of Species.* New American Library, Penguin Group, New York, 2003. (First published in Great Britain in 1859.)

46 Lex Friedman Podcast, episode 87. https://youtu.be/5f-JlzBuUUU?si=0KaBjs3CApVipSe4, interview with Richard Dawkins. Lex does in other podcast-episodes also memorably interview both Richard Wrangham and Roger Penrose, whom both are mentioned within this book.

47 Wrangham, Richard. *The Goodness Paradox. How Evolution made Us both More and Less Violent.* UK, Profile Books Ltd, 2020.

48 Anders Hansen is a Swedish writer, psychiatrist, Bachelor of Economics, Lecturer, and host of National Televisions series such as the one in which he interviews Professor Richard Wrangham. https://www.svtplay.se/din-hjarna Episode 4.

Chapter 17

49 Cliff, Jimmy. *The Harder They Come, The Harder They Fall.* The song appeared in the Jamaican crime movie *The Harder They Come,* 1972, directed by Perry Henzell and co-written by Trevor. D. Rhone. Jimmy Cliff played the main character

in this highly memorable film that kick-started the Jamaican Reggae boom.

Acknowledgments

50   Penrose, Roger. English mathematician and theoretical physicist, born in 1931, has written several books, whereof *The Emperors' New Mind* is one. I have not read his books but listened to several lectures and interviews on the internet. To everyone who wants to rub their intellects against some profound thought-investigation, let me recommend viewing an interview broadcasted by *The Institute of Art (iai)* in 2020, named, 'Roger Penrose, Gravity, Hawking Points, and Twistor Theory'. https://youtu.be/9Gl8pwY2kW8?si=27YKbRYdS3MKCdT1. And the interview made by Andrea Morris for *Variable Minds,* in 2023, named 'Roger Penrose's Mind Bending Theory of Reality'. https://youtu.be/itLIM38k2r0?si=-x4HmIiSH-gaK5gS

Additional note

51   I like to end this Notes and Bibliography-section, by mentioning yet another spokesman for Vedanta and the Vedic wisdom tradition who has just recently come to my attention, and whom I definitely will return to in days to come. His name is Swami A. Parthasarathy, born in 1927. He is the leader of an organization called Vedanta World, www. vedantaworld.org, including *The Vedanta Academy* outside Mumbai. Swamiji is a highly acclaimed teacher and lecturer both in the world of business and in the world of spiritual growth. There is much to be said about him, as a sportsman, an entrepreneur, a businessman, an author, and more, but I foremostly like to draw upon that he puts clear emphasize on the power of the intellect. He says that our intellect, when used in a clear and rightful way, is our best means, and our sharpest tool to attain liberation from worldly bondage and personal suffering. I find it interesting

because it reminds me about the message given by the infinity principle. The infinity principle too, addresses our intellects. It is possible to understand the deep riddles about existence and go on to use that understanding in a beneficial way in the world. The intelligent mind and the intellect are not the same thing here. The intellect can control the mind so that the mind does not jump out of control and cause harm. That is an interesting way to address the ongoing confusion in the world. In the US, Gautam Jain, (Gautamji), senior protégé of Swami Parthasarathy further teaches this line of thought. www.vedantausa.org

Printed in the United States
by Baker & Taylor Publisher Services